Ruth Orkin

Introduction by Anne Morin

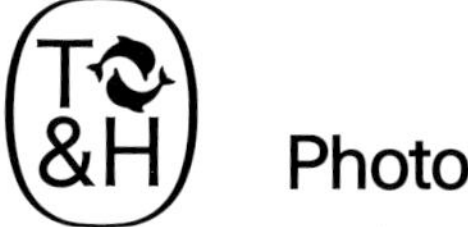

Photofile

The Pulse of Time

In the early 20th century, the United States was not an easy place for a woman seeking to pursue a career in film. The Directors Guild of America admitted its first woman, the filmmaker Dorothy Arzner (1897–1979) in 1938. She remained the DGA's only female member for twenty-eight years until Ida Lupino (1918–1995) joined in 1966. The American Society of Cinematographers did not admit its first woman, Brianne Murphy (1933–2003) until 1980, a staggering fifty years after its establishment. Clearly, a profound gender bias plagued the American movie industry blocking the career paths of most women interested in film.

In the world of cinema, as in photography, women were only trusted to carry out minor tasks related to production, such as developing negatives, film editing or retouching – in other words, jobs that were in some ways reminiscent of domestic labour. It was rare to find a woman involved in the work behind the camera rather than in front of it. There are a few exceptions scattered throughout the history of film, such as Alice Guy (1873–1968), recognized as the first female director; Lois Weber (1879–1939), an actress, soprano and pianist who became one of the most prolific filmmakers of the early 20th century; Frances Marion (1888–1973), the first female screenwriter to receive an Oscar, for her work on the film *The Big House* (1930); and Maya Deren (1917–61), who was a major player in redefining experimental American cinema. But from the start, the American film industry was not inclined toward gender equality.

Ruth Orkin (1921–85) initially had to give up on her dream of being a filmmaker, or, at least, she had to take a different route, in order to pursue this dream in a different form. It was probably this setback that allowed her to develop such a distinctive visual language as a photographer. The daughter of Mary Ruby, a silent-film actress, and Samuel Orkin, an entrepreneur in the model boat industry, she grew up behind the scenes of Hollywood in the 1920s and 1930s. She first became interested in photography at the age of ten, when she started experimenting with her first camera, 'a 39-cent Univex', as she recalled. But Orkin's true passion was cinema, the moving image and the passing of time. In the early 1940s she worked as a messenger girl at Metro-Goldwyn-Mayer, an eager, enthusiastic young woman running from one department to the next, making sure to take the time to look closely and learn many lessons that she would draw on in her still photography. She also studied photojournalism at Los Angeles City College in the early 1940s and then embarked on a career in reportage photography, working with major illustrated magazines such as *Life*, *Look* and *Ladies Home Journal*.

This fascination with the power of cinema remained a constant presence throughout Orkin's work, and it was this sense of having missed the opportunity to pursue her vocation that led her to invent an entirely new language that stood at the crossroads between photography and cinema. A language that exists in the space between the moving image and the still image, neither one nor the other, and creates a constant dialogue between these two converging treatments of time. Throughout her career, these two concepts were constantly seeping into one another, intertwining until they came to form the basis of her visual language.

From her earliest pictures, the spirit of cinema appears in a variety of forms. It is hidden in the tiny fissures in a photogram and imbues the image with multiple layers, where the flow of movement creates a rhythm. A spark, a trigger, a trace that creates a filmlike effect, a simulated sense of time passing, like a special effect in a movie, like an editing glitch. And what does it matter if these glitches are too visible? 'Movies arise out of magic; from below the world,' Stanley Cavell wrote in *The World Viewed* (1971),[1] and therefore what matters is our willingness to believe.

In her process, Orkin returned again and again to ideas of seriality and intermittency, where time can be reshaped, moulded, expanded. In her pictures, time is plural. She brings together and breaks down different units of time, each one distinct from the others. The most basic mechanism that she uses to simulate time consists of including in a picture two figures that are very similar, almost identical, but just different enough that the viewer is not entirely taken in. Through this doubling of the subject, Orkin seems to want to convey a sort of simultaneity that tricks the eye, creating the illusion of movement. The two figures make the same gesture, adopt the same pose or posture, with only a small difference, and it is this dissonance, this small gap between the two, that creates a sense of time. The simple juxtaposition of these figures breathes a sense of temporality into her photographs.

This sense of temporality can also be felt in groups of images over varying spans of time. In what could have become her first road movie, created in 1939 when she cycled across the USA from Los Angeles to New York City, Orkin kept a diary that itself became a kind of film sequence, a documentary that recorded this journey in a chronological manner. Inspired by the scrapbooks and albums that her mother kept from films that she'd worked on, and using the same approach of adding handwritten captions, Orkin placed photographic images in a narrative sequence that draws on the storyboards used in filmmaking. The length of the story is the length of the journey. Once again, she cuts through the continuity, and the vignette-like images punctuate the space that is created, like stills from a movie that never happened, or at least was never filmed.

When Orkin moved to New York in 1943, she worked as a nightclub photographer, finessed her way into the Tanglewood Music Festival, and shot iconic photos of Leonard Bernstein, Isaac Stern, and others. To protest the government's crackdown on artists and writers suspected of being communists, she also joined the Photo League in 1950, in a show of solidarity. It was here that she met Morris Engel, her future husband and collaborator, and his friend, the 19-year-old *Look* magazine staff photographer, Stanley Kubrick. She started doing more work for major magazines and that was when her career began to take off. She became one of the women of the moment and was recognized as a skilled photojournalist.

In New York, she was immediately struck by the city as a visual space, a place of visual stimuli driven by an unceasing rhythm that continued night and day. It held a true fascination for Orkin, and had a profound influence on her visual language.

While the photography of the early 20th century was exploring a world in constant motion, the medium itself also became more mobile thanks to new portable technology. Since the turn of the 20th century, Paris, New York, London and the capital cities of the world had been undergoing significant changes in their urban environments. Modernity was taking hold, time was moving faster, traffic was speeding up and becoming more congested, crowds never stopped moving, department stores sprang up and were transformed into blazing visions of light. The visual language was changing, with both the gaze and the viewer travelling faster through an ever-moving world. In this context, photography became a vital tool for breaking down time and capturing what could not be perceived by the eye alone. Points of view began to move away from the centre and the field of vision became wider, with more unusual framings: high-angle shots, low-angle shots, close-ups, and depth of field. Photographers felt time pushing forward and captured a sense of time passing within an image, without pushing it far enough to encroach on cinema.

It was against this backdrop of experimentation in the world of photography that Orkin appeared on the New York art scene. She became captivated by the small things that she discovered on the streets of Manhattan. A gesture, a pose, a look, a sort of fluid lyricism that infused the world of everyday people, deeply rooted in daily life, a sense of immutability and humbleness. Pictures that are 'disconcerting in their simplicity, because they seem to show nothing'[2] – these are the words of Hervé Guibert describing André Kertész's last exhibition in Paris in 1980, but they could equally be applied to Orkin's work. In her creative vision, there is no sign of a society taking great strides forward into the modern era, or of the city sprouting toward the sky, the growing, overflowing power that Berenice Abbott had documented so well a few years earlier in her series *Changing New York* (1939).

Orkin leaned into this world, quite literally: she observed it through her window, transcribing the unceasing dance of the passers-by, who, when viewed from above, looked like tiny moving particles that together mapped out the flow of movement on the city's streets. It was only this bird's-eye view that allowed her to see and understand this complex phenomenon of drift and motion, which was otherwise invisible. In this series of images, called *From Above* (ills. 7–10), which were collected and published as a book in 1978, she is the spectator of her own cinematic vision, which she renders in its entirety. She focuses her gaze on the constantly moving city, returning to the same themes over and over again. She tirelessly repeats the same gesture, probably driven by the visual memory etched into her retina.

Children are a constant presence in her photographs, probably for the same reason they often appear in the work of Helen Levitt, who explained: 'Adults are always sitting down or standing up. Children adopt a thousand different poses. If I'm fascinated by them, it's not because they are cute, as people say, but because they are never still. They have emotions, they are imaginative, active, they play, and they are constantly changing how they relate to each other in their games, they dress up, they come together in different compositions.'[3]

Orkin spent time with the children in her neighbourhood, who sometimes became the actors in small sketches or film sequences like those in the series *The Card Players* (ills. 59–64) and *Jimmy Tells a Story* (ills. 45–50), which both consist of groups of six images. Orkin used her camera to take photographs that have the feel of cinema; the repetition creates not only differences, but also small gaps in between the images that generate a sense of time passing as you move from one to the next, creating the illusion of a continuous thread. The use of repeated images creates a rhythm, a beat, a sense of movement, and in this way, her pictures take on a temporal dimension and come to form a kind of filmic narrative. What counts, as Gilles Deleuze wrote in *Cinema 2: The Time-Image*, is 'the interstice between images, between two images: a spacing which means that each image is plucked from the void and falls back into it.'[4] A space where the image is in flux, a space that relies on the observer's gaze to recreate the motion, like a zoetrope.

In 1951, Orkin travelled around Israel with the Israel Philharmonic Orchestra, shooting their performances as a reporter for *Life*

magazine. A few weeks later, before returning to New York,
she stopped off in Italy, visiting several cities, including Florence. By
chance, she met Ninalee Craig, known as Jinx, an art history student
and fellow American, who became the main subject of *American Girl
in Italy* (ills. 29, 31–34). This series of photographs, originally called
Don't Be Afraid to Travel Alone, depicts their experiences of travelling
alone as women in post-war Europe. Orkin experimented with a form
that would make this series one of the most memorable of her career.
She approached the subject by adopting a genre that was very popular
in Italy in the 1940s: the photo story. This new kind of narrative,
which combined text and photographs, first appeared in Italy in 1946
and was commonly used by Italian post-war magazines. The way it
was made was reminiscent of silent films, while its form was more
like a comic strip. A symbol of the industry surrounding popular
culture, the photo story marked the start of a new era. Photography
followed in the footsteps of cinema, as the temporality of film
influenced the photographic process.

Orkin did not hesitate to embrace the photo story format,
producing a sequence that was both theatrical and literary. She
created a web of chance occurrences that coalesced to form a central
narrative thread acted out by the protagonist, Jinx, an actress for
the occasion. Jinx emphasized the performative element with her
expressions, which verged on caricature and imbued the image with
meaning, while still leaving the observer the task of interpreting its
intention. After this sequence, there was only one more step that
Orkin needed to take in order to establish herself in the world of
cinema: making a feature-length film.

In 1953, Orkin and the American photographer and director Morris
Engel co-produced, co-directed, and, along with writer Ray Ashley,
co-wrote the American independent film classic, *Little Fugitive*. Not
only did Orkin take a number of photographs of the shoot, but she
also left an undeniable imprint on almost every aspect of the film
itself, including the editing.

Winner of the Silver Lion at the Venice Film Festival and
nominated for an Academy Award for Best Motion Picture Story

for Ashley, Engel and Orkin, *Little Fugitive* had a profound influence on generations of filmmakers, especially on the conventions and approaches of the French New Wave. It is considered one of the landmark films of modern cinema. The film tells the story of a young boy of seven in New York in the early 1950s. After his older brother, Lennie, plays a practical joke on him, making him think he has shot him dead – tomato ketchup rubbed on his T-shirt is enough to convince the boy – young Joey runs away and wanders through the city alone. He arrives at the amusement park on Coney Island, where he starts to enjoy himself, forgetting why he has run away, as if the bustle of the fair has created an altered state of consciousness. The young boy becomes the incarnation of the present moment, experiencing it in all its intensity, hardly noticing anything else. The experience of the present moment is all that counts in this section of the film. In an article published in *Cahiers du Cinéma* (no. 31, January 1954), André Bazin argued that the radical novelty of *Little Fugitive* lies in the fact that its subject, at its most basic, is created by the structure of the narrative itself, and that it comes close to the ideal of a film with no screenplay at all, where the drama is solely born from the way in which the present moment unfolds. The wanderings of the child actor are what drive the film, not the other way around.

François Truffaut took inspiration from this story for his 1959 film *The 400 Blows*, in which the character of Antoine Doinel, a teenage rebel, runs away after a series of tragic events. Jean-Luc Godard's 1960 film *Breathless*, which stars Jean-Paul Belmondo and Jean Seberg, was also inspired by *Little Fugitive*. Michel, a young criminal, steals a car in Marseille to go to Paris, but he is pursued by the police and kills an officer. The idea of the protagonist performing an action, running away and then wandering forms the narrative arc of the film, recalling the figure of the *flâneur*, popularized by Walter Benjamin in his discussion of the poetry of Charles Baudelaire.[5]

Throughout her career, Orkin remained fascinated by and involved with the world of film, shooting portraits of some of the most famous actors and actresses of the day. Her gallery of subjects included Alfred Hitchcock, Vittorio De Sica (ill. 35), Lauren Bacall (ill. 38), Humphrey

Bogart, Marlon Brando and Woody Allen. The long list also featured other famous names from the worlds of film, photography, music and even science, such as Robert Capa (ill. 40), Leonard Bernstein (ill. 67) and Albert Einstein (ill. 39). All of these portraits show how Orkin was able to create a sense of complicity, even a kind of intimacy, so that her subjects could lose themselves in the moment when their picture was being taken, allowing something spontaneous to emerge, something true that went beyond the concept of intimate resemblance that characterized Nadar's portraits in the late 19th century. Orkin had a gift for allowing what she considered truly important to shine through: humanity and charisma, no matter whom she was photographing. For her, her subject's social status made no difference, and that was undoubtedly what allowed her to always see life up close and reproduce it in its entirety.

Orkin's work earned her a place in the history of photography, in its gaps and the places where it intersects with other disciplines. It was the fact that she was at first thwarted in following her dream of becoming a cinematographer that allowed her to open herself up to other ways of understanding images that existed on the borderline between worlds. Orkin's work is permeated by a sense of the struggles she had to go through to take up her rightful place, without ever giving up on what drove her: the desire to tell stories through images. She had to break down her approach and remake it anew, creating space for her artistic vision. That is the true legacy that she left for the generations that followed, who have picked up where she left off.

Anne Morin

Notes

1   Stanley Cavell, *The World Viewed: Reflections on the Ontology of Film*, Cambridge, MA: Harvard University Press, 1979, p. 39.

2   Hervé Guibert, *La photo, inéluctablement*, Paris: Gallimard, 1999, p. 273.

3   'Les enfants d'Helen Levitt', interview published in *Le Monde*, 26 March 1981.

4   Gilles Deleuze, *Cinema 2: The Time-Image*, Minneapolis: University of Minnesota Press, 2001, p. 179.

5   Walter Benjamin, 'Baudelaire, or the streets of Paris', published posthumously in *Paris, Capital of the 19th Century* (1938)

1. 'Bicycle on a hill in San Francisco',
from the series *Bicycle Trip*, 1939.

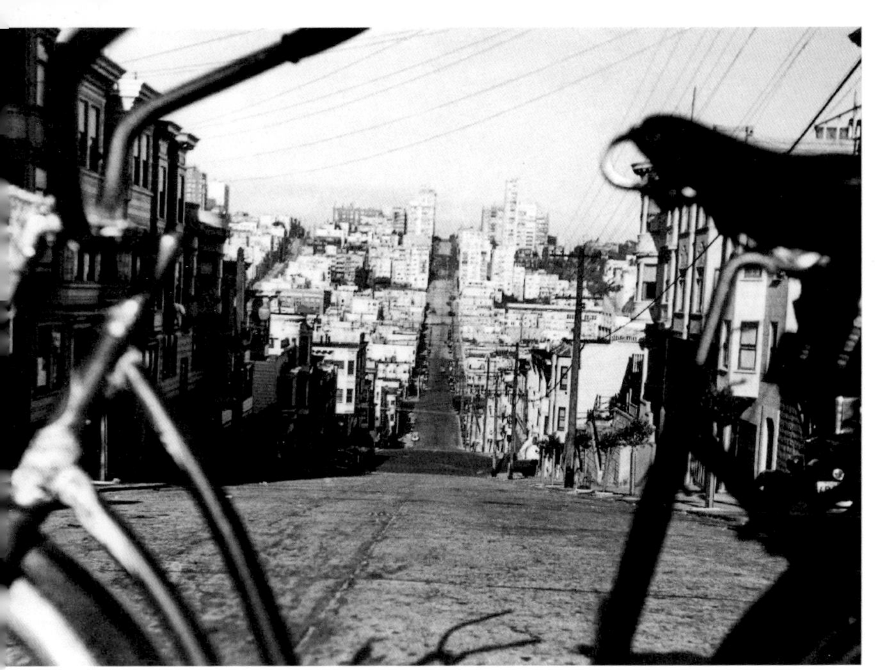

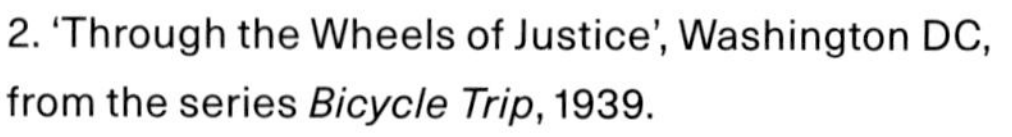
2. 'Through the Wheels of Justice', Washington DC,
from the series *Bicycle Trip*, 1939.

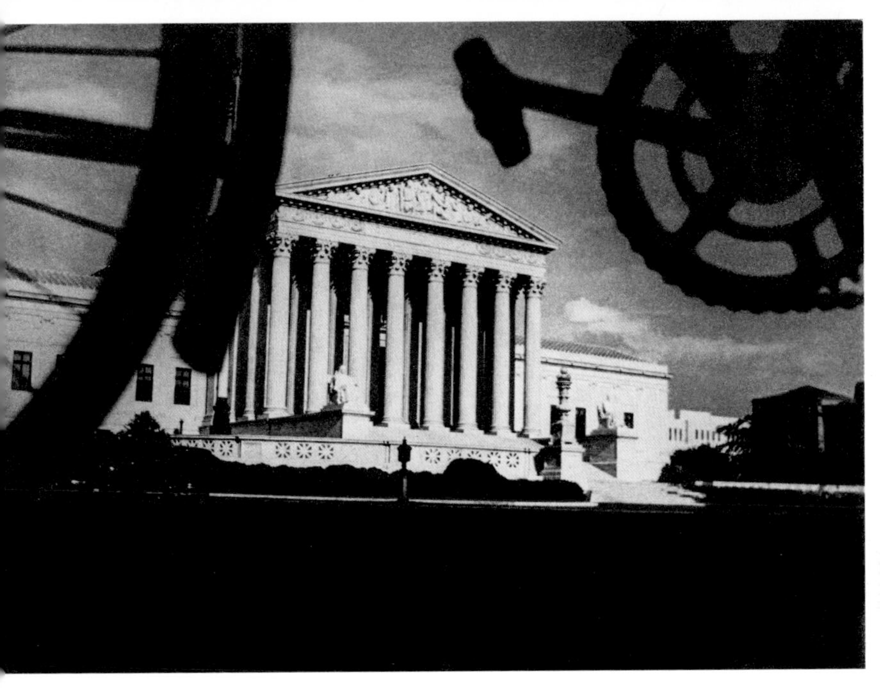

3. 'Through the dashboard', USA,
from the series *Bicycle Trip*, 1939.

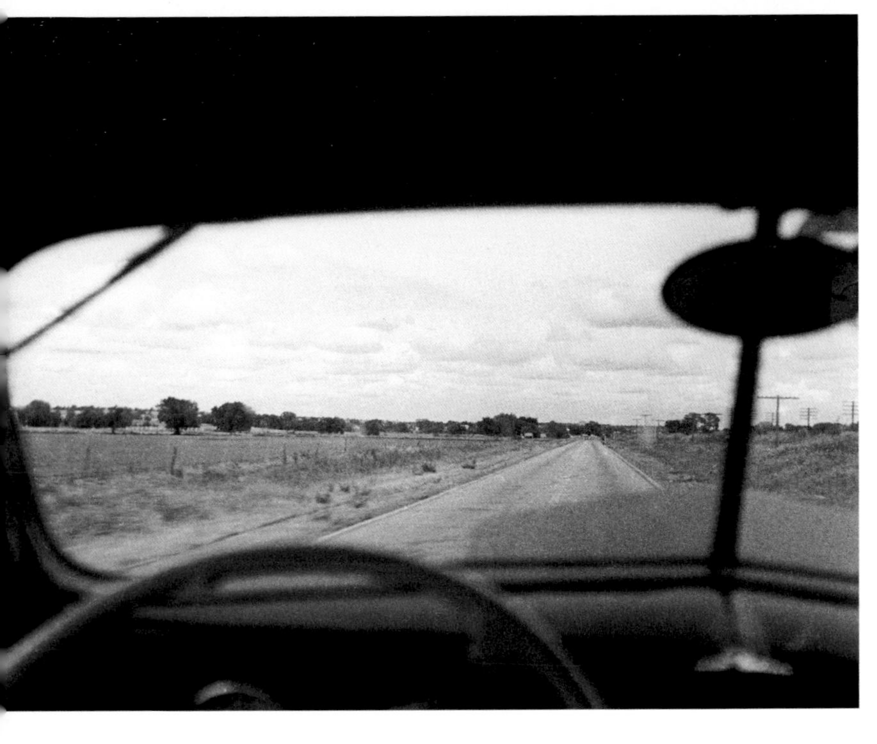

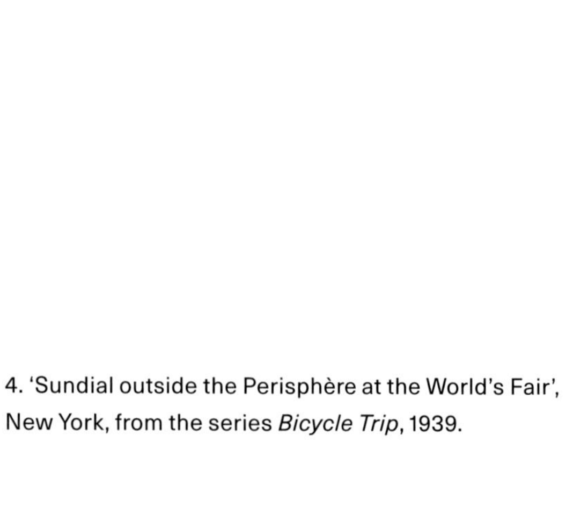

4. 'Sundial outside the Perisphère at the World's Fair',
New York, from the series *Bicycle Trip*, 1939.

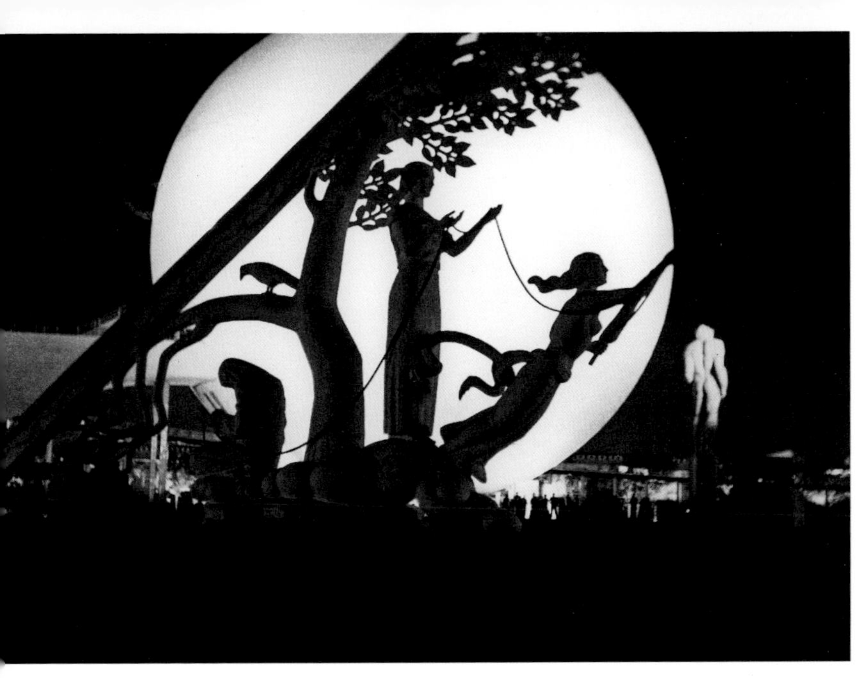

5. 'New York World's Fair by night', from
the series *Bicycle Trip*, 1939. Vintage print.

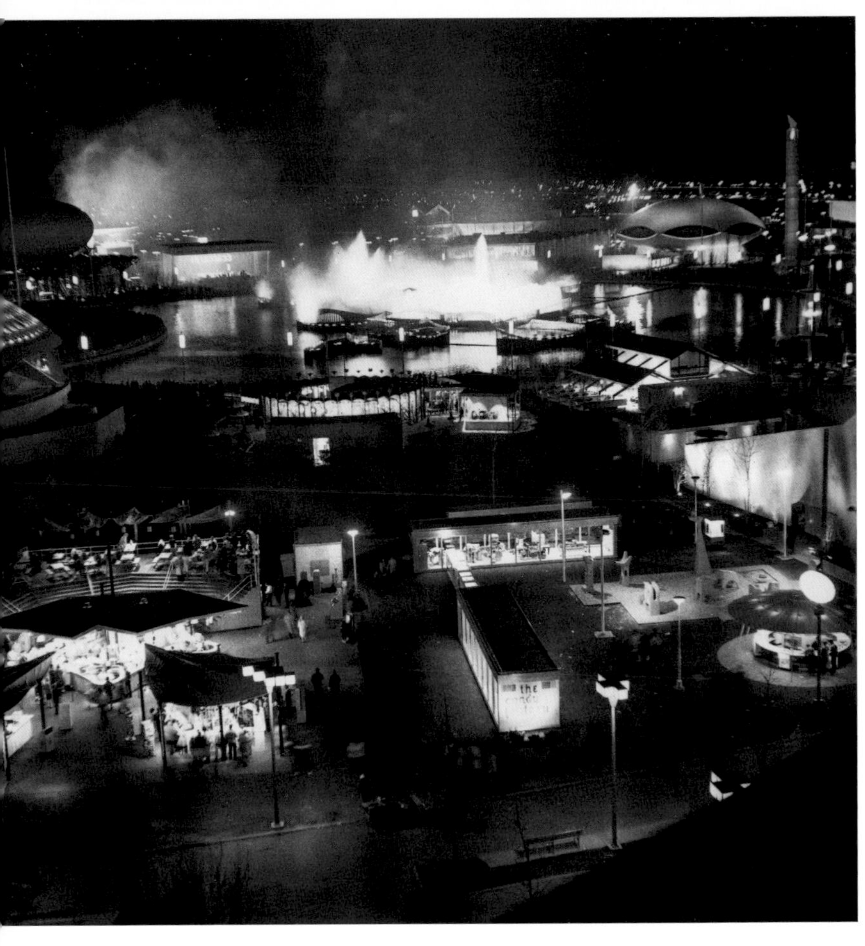

6. White stoops, West 88th Street, New York, 1952.

Overleaf:
7. Girls twirling, New York, from the series *From Above*, 1948.

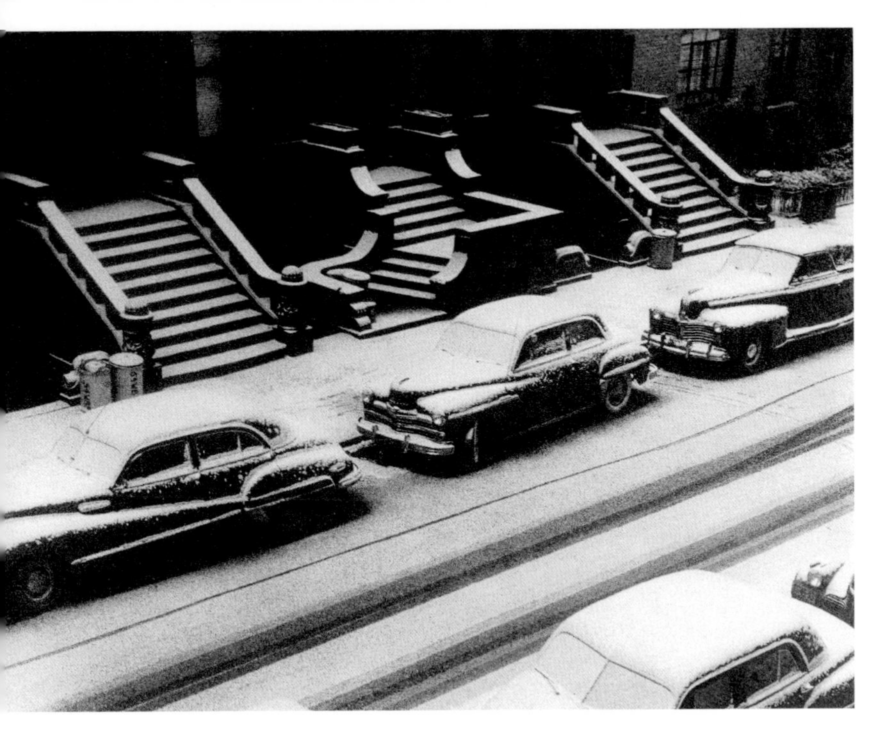

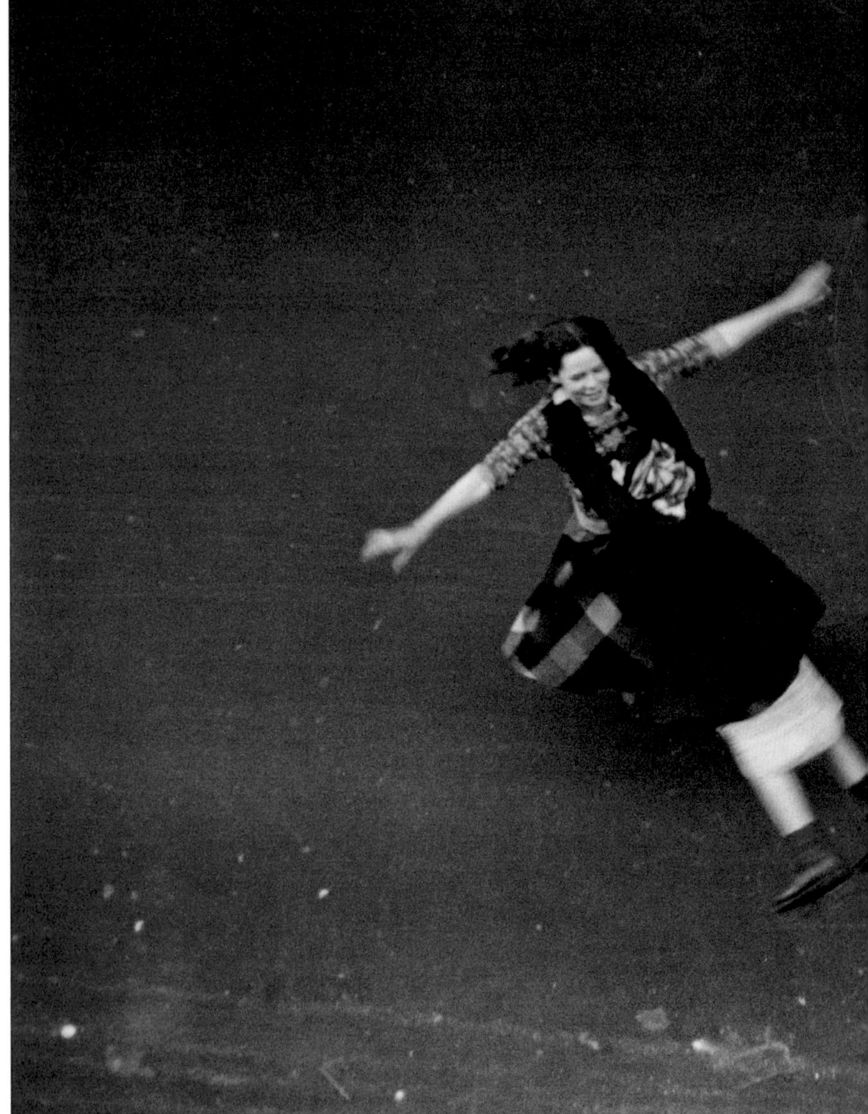

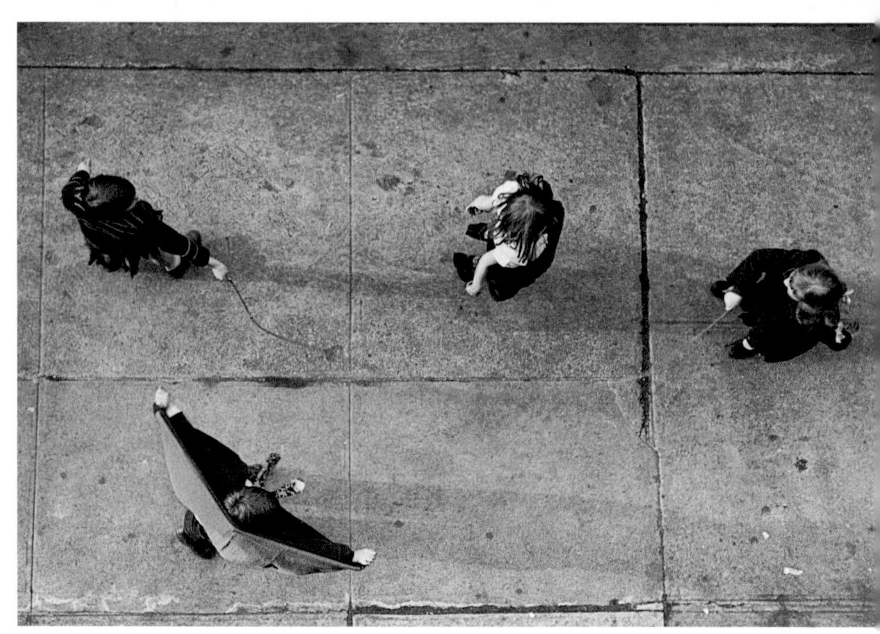

8. 'Girls jumping rope', New York,
from the series *From Above*, late 1940s.

9. 'Mattress', New York, from the series
From Above, 1940s.

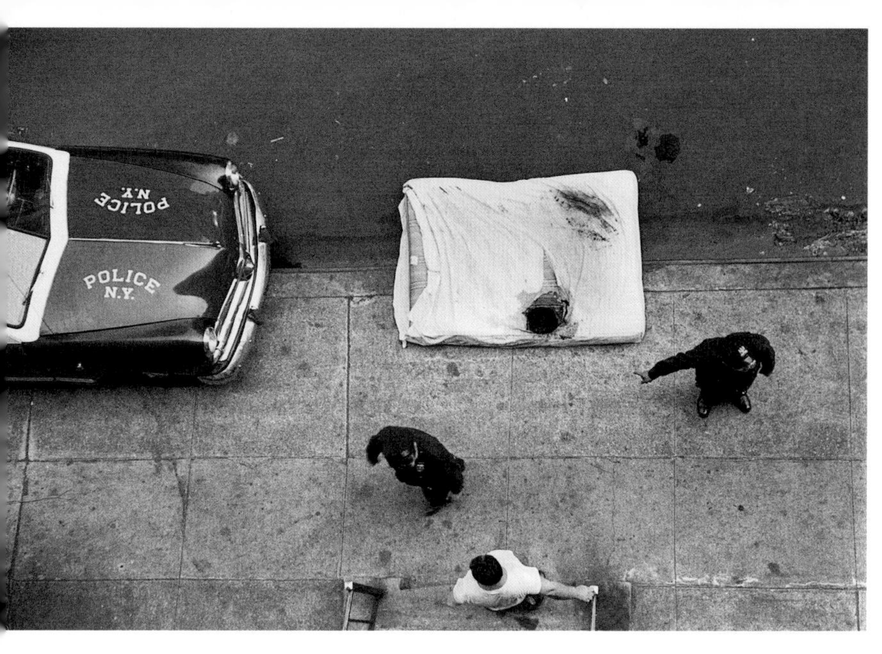

POLICE
N.Y.
POLICE
N.Y.

10. 'Couple', New York, from
the series *From Above*, 1940s.

Overleaf:
11. People lying on Tanglewood Lawn,
Lenox, Massachusetts, 1948.

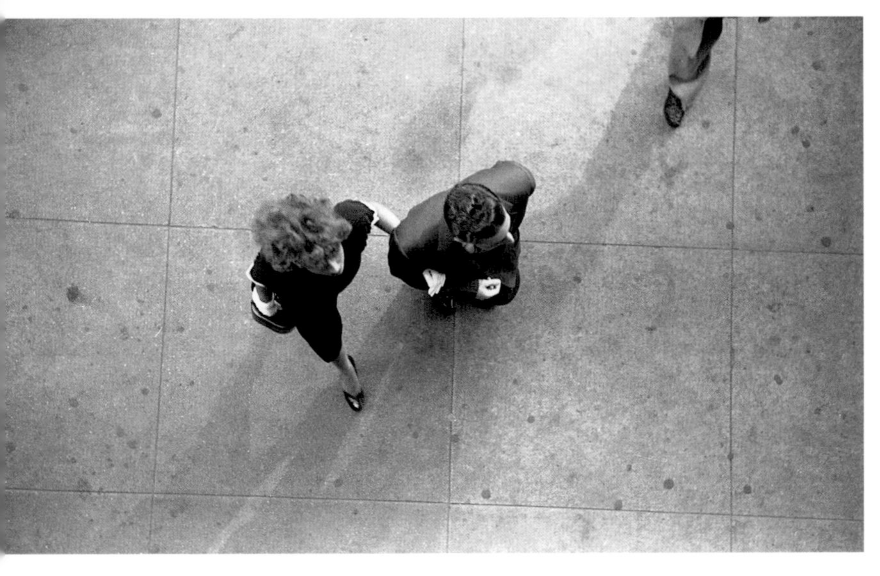

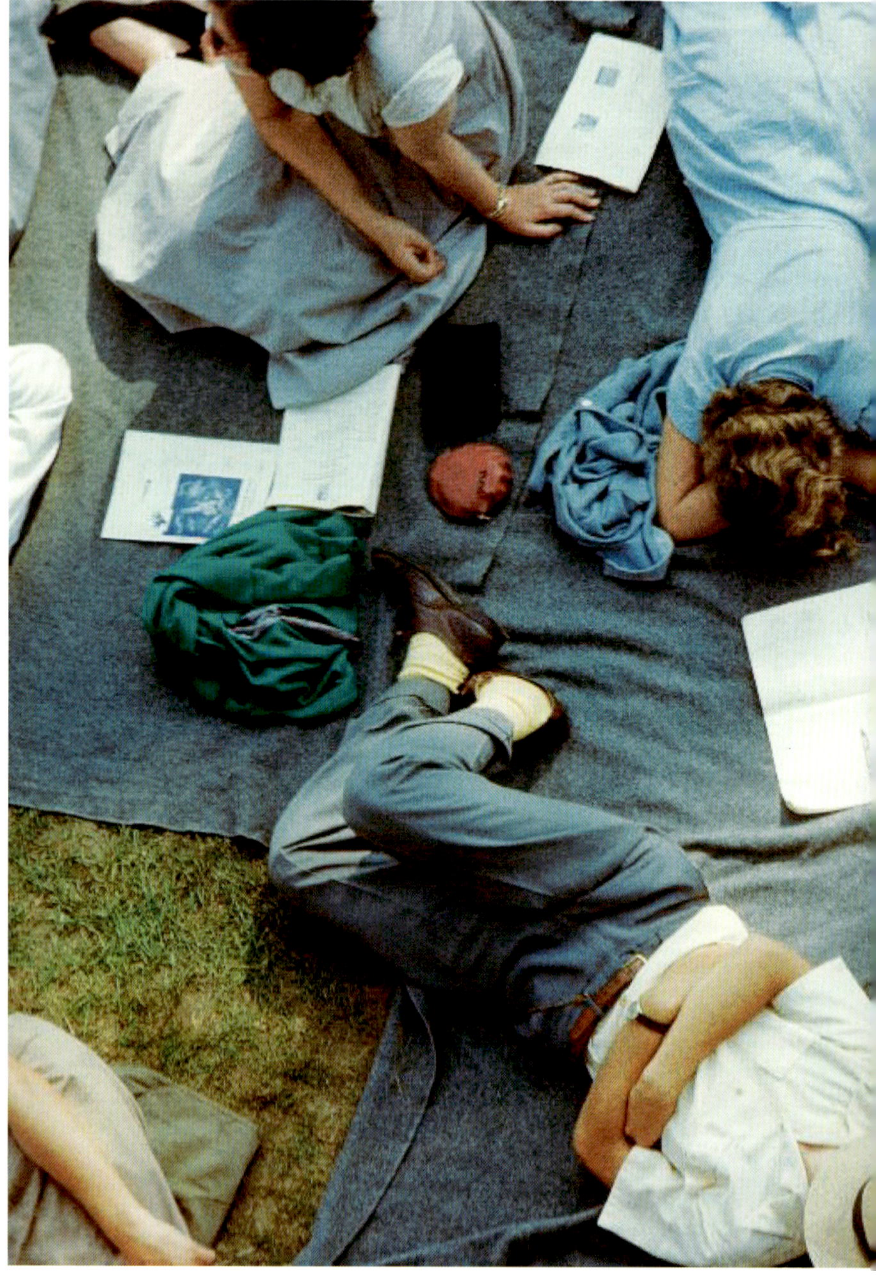

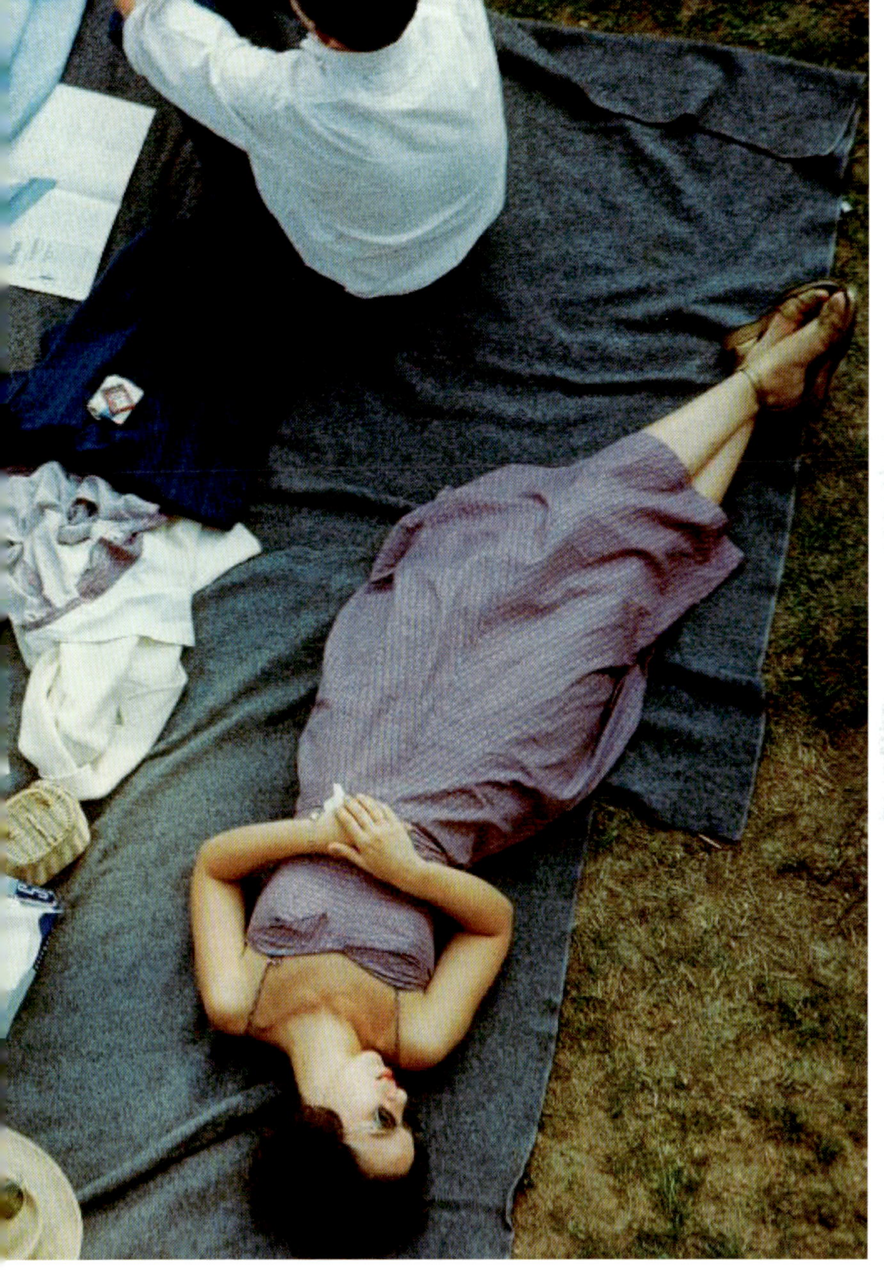

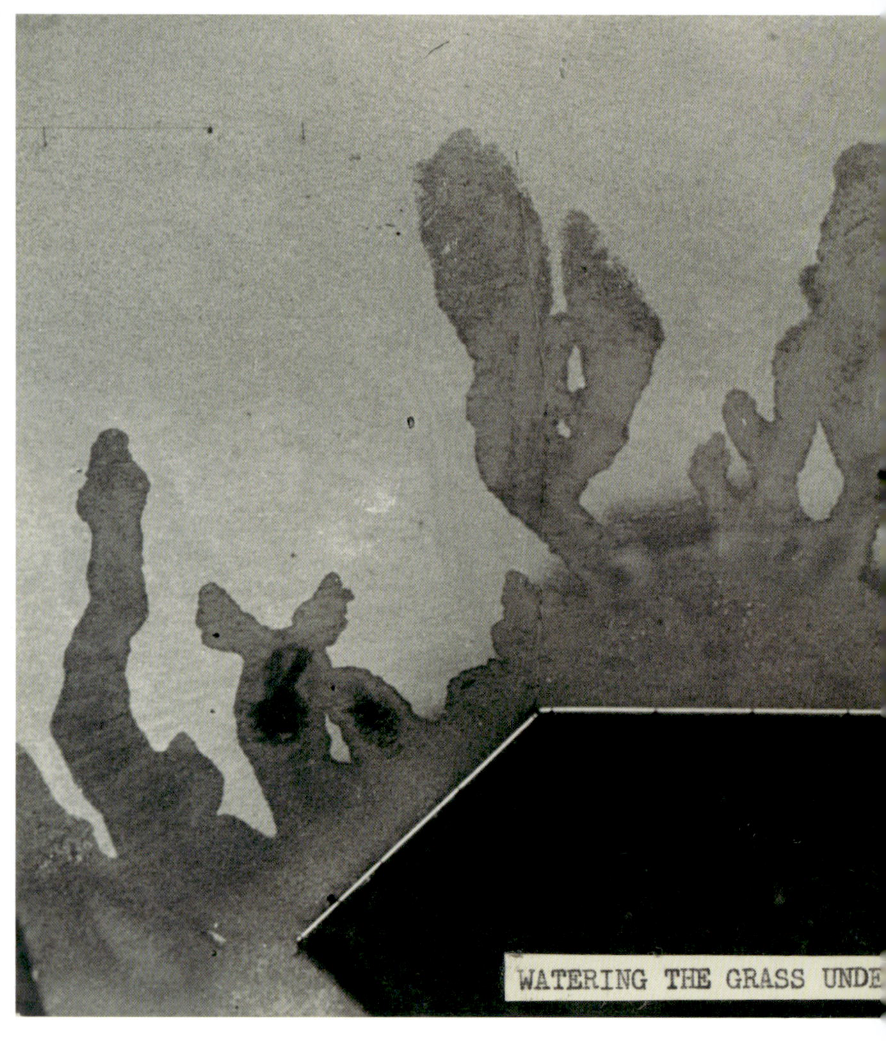

WATERING THE GRASS UNDE

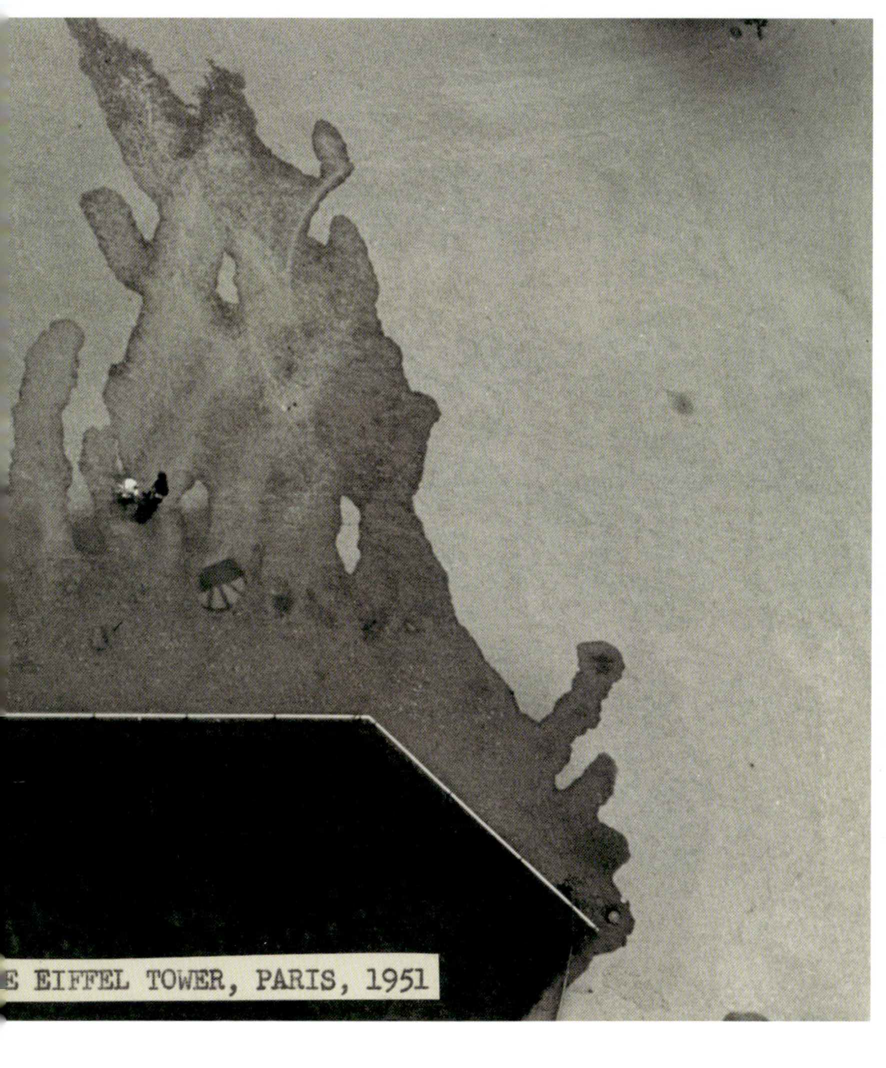

E EIFFEL TOWER, PARIS, 1951

Previous pages:

12. Watering the grass under the Eiffel Tower, Paris, 1951.

13. Starlight Roof, New York, 1950.

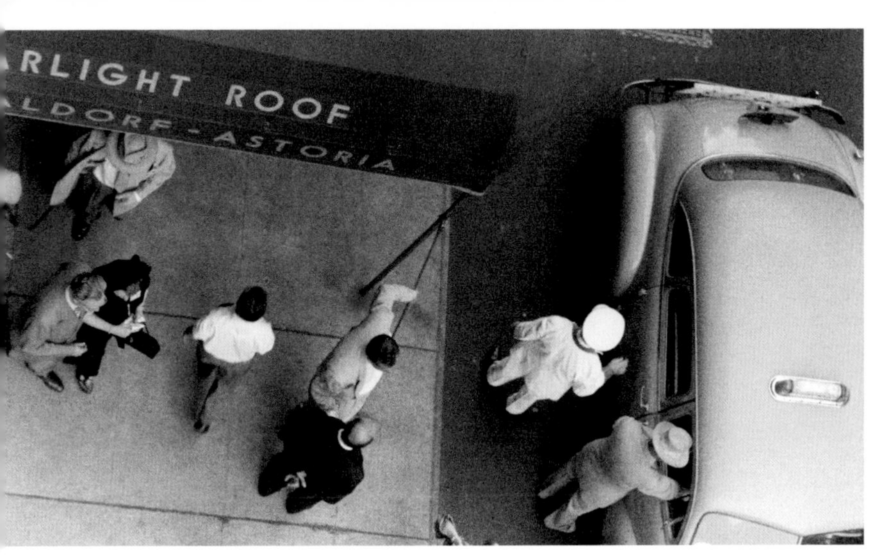

RLIGHT ROOF
LDORF-ASTORIA

14. Taxis in the parking lot at Tavern on the Green,
New York, late 1960s.

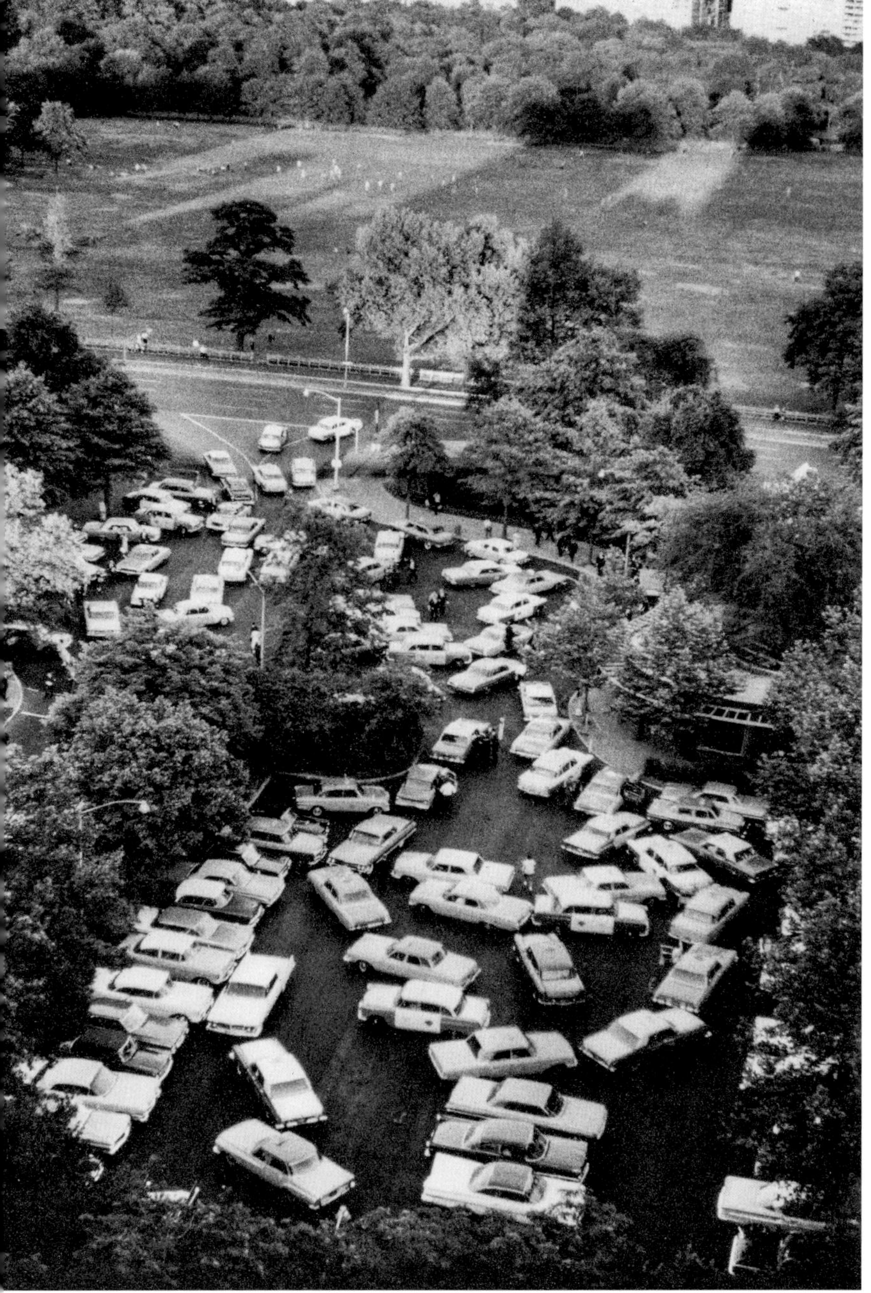

15. Man in rain, West 88th Street, New York, 1952.

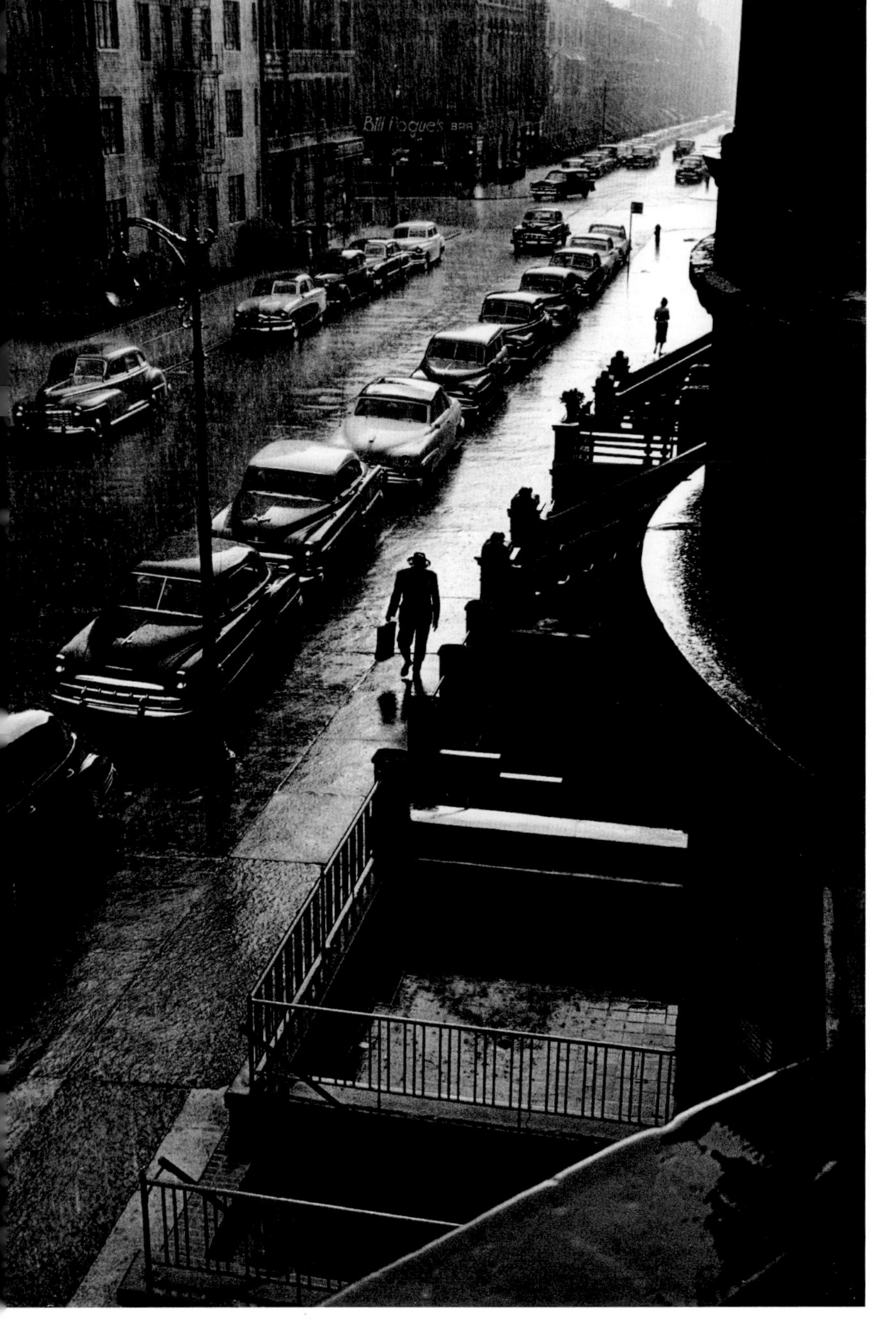
Bill Rogue's BAR

16. Women walking, Midtown, New York, mid-1940s.

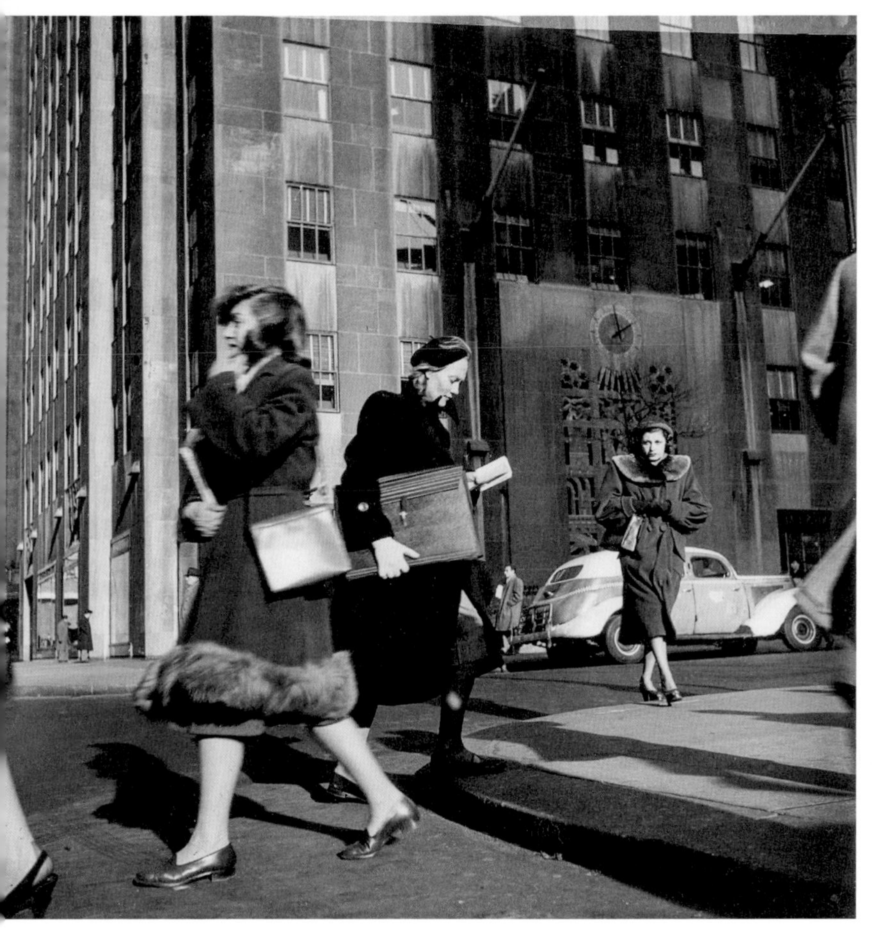

17. Spencer Tracy on location, New York, 1950s.

Overleaf:
18. Waiting to cross Sixth Avenue, New York, late 1940s.

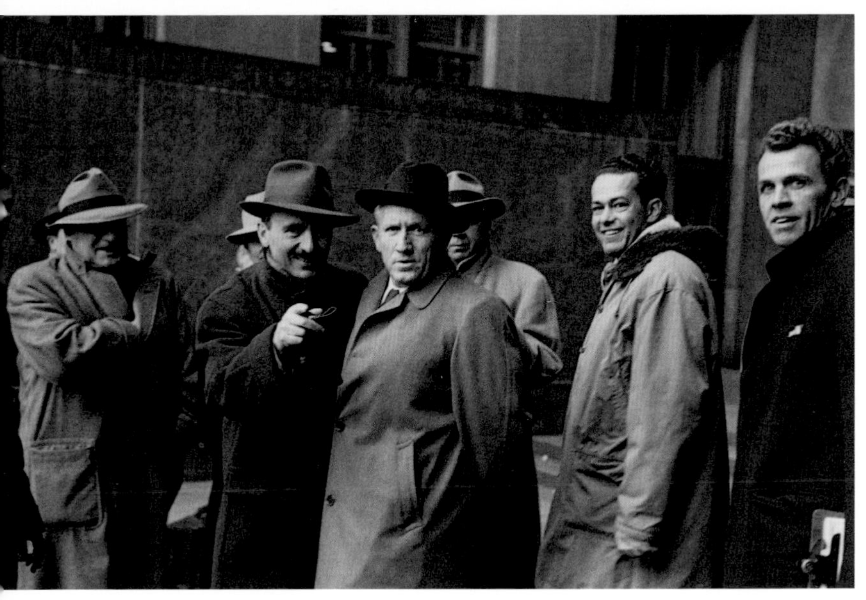

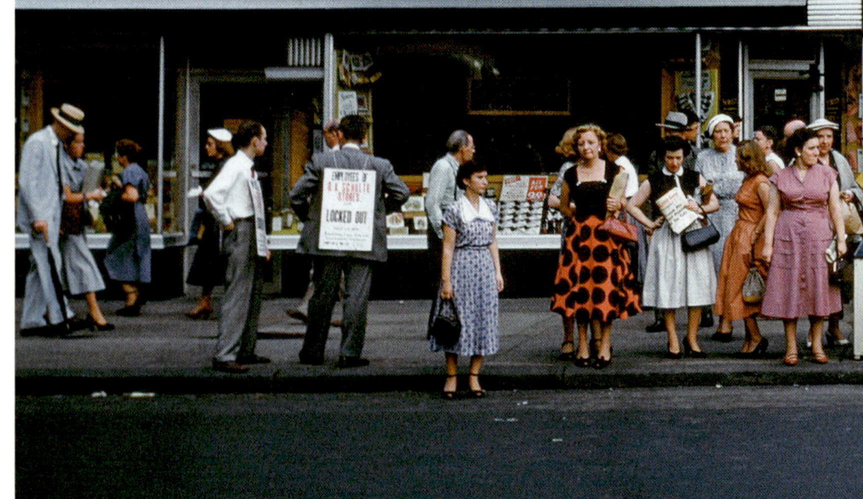

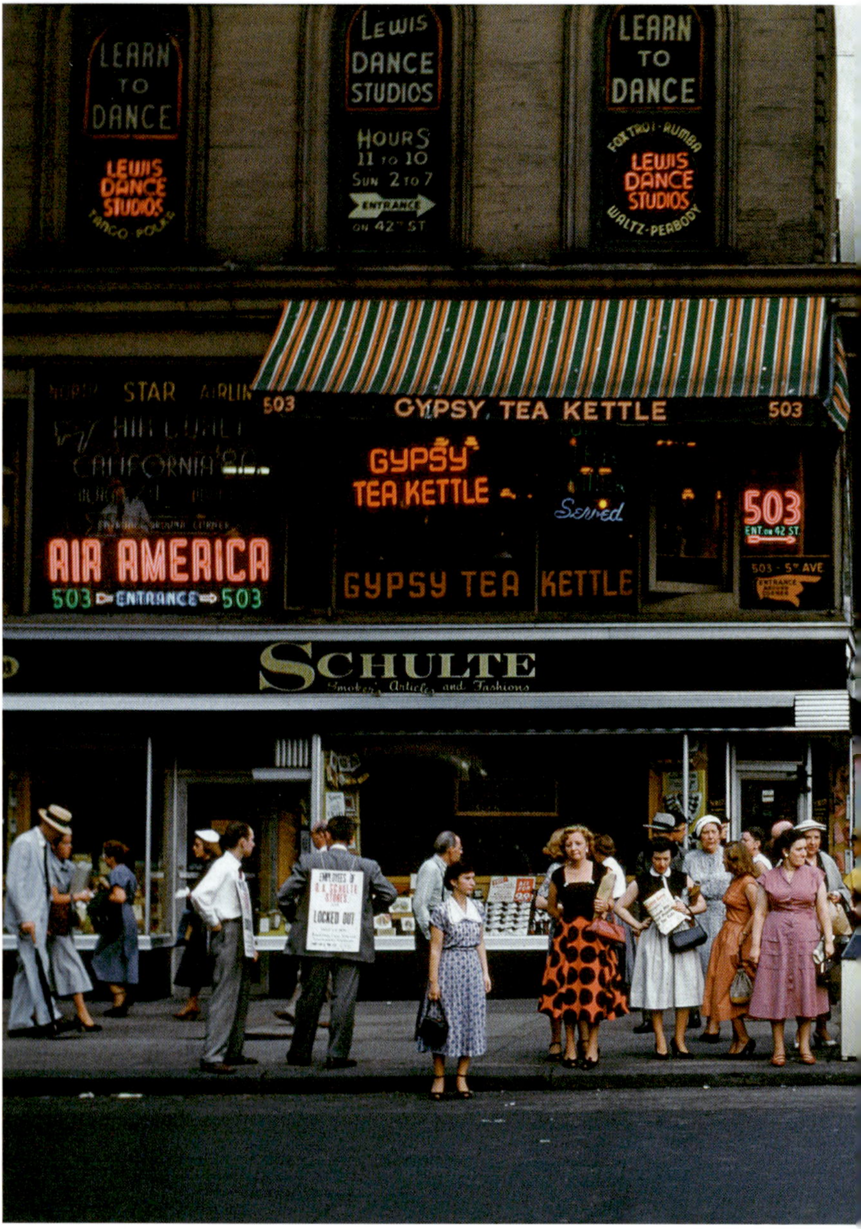

LEARN
TO
DANCE
LEWIS
DANCE
STUDIOS
TANGO-POLKA
LEWIS
DANCE
STUDIOS
HOURS
11 TO 10
SUN 2 TO 7
ENTRANCE
ON 42ND ST
LEARN
TO
DANCE
FOXTROT-RUMBA
LEWIS
DANCE
STUDIOS
WALTZ-PEABODY
STAR AIRLIN
CALIFORNIA
AIR AMERICA
503 ENTRANCE 503
503
GYPSY, TEA KETTLE
503
GYPSY
TEA KETTLE
Served
GYPSY TEA KETTLE
503
ENT. ON 42 ST.
503 - 5TH AVE
ENTRANCE
AROUND CORNER
SCHULTE
Smoker's Articles and Fashions
EMPLOYEES OF
D. A. SCHULTE
STORES
LOCKED OUT

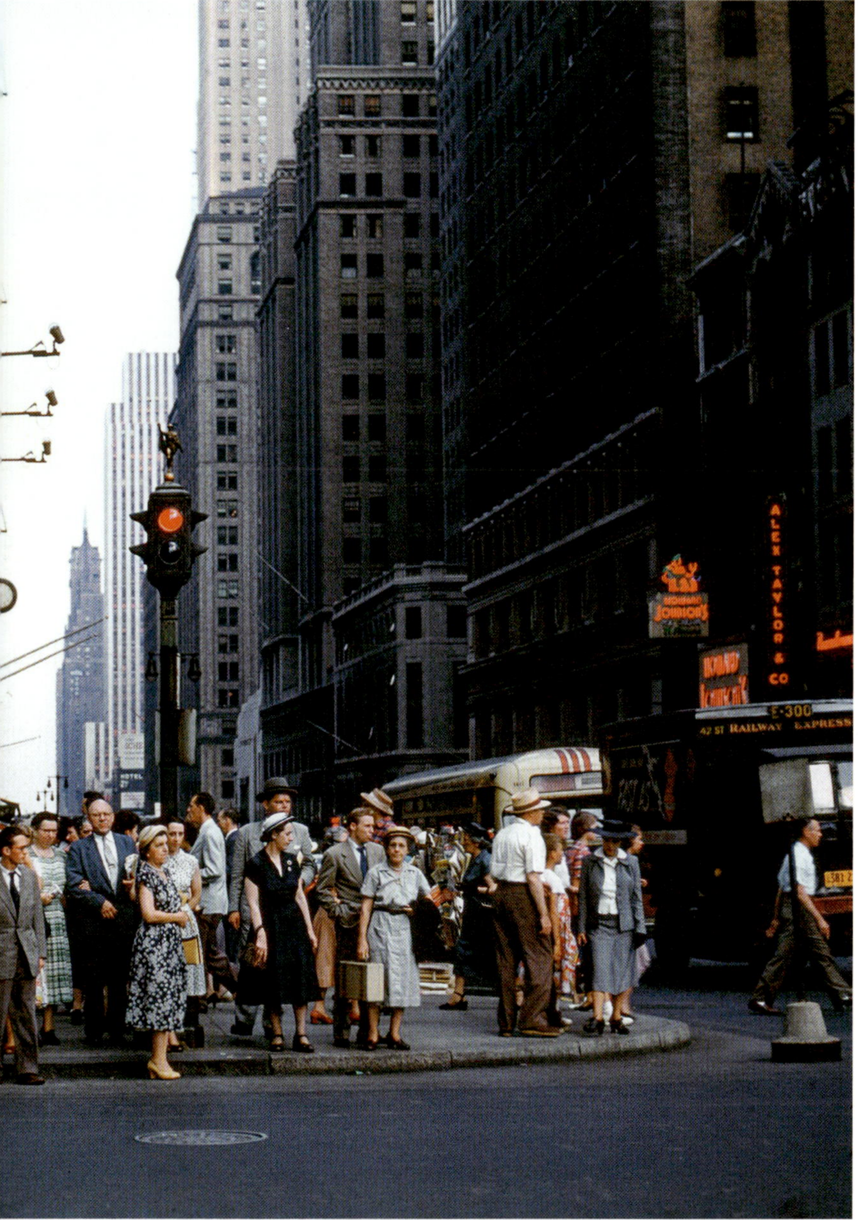

HOWARD
JOHNSON'S
ALEX TAYLOR & CO
HOWARD CLOTHES
E·300
42 ST RAILWAY EXPRESS

19. VE Day, Times Square, New York, 1945.

Overleaf:
20. Members of the Women's Army Corps, Arkansas, 1943.

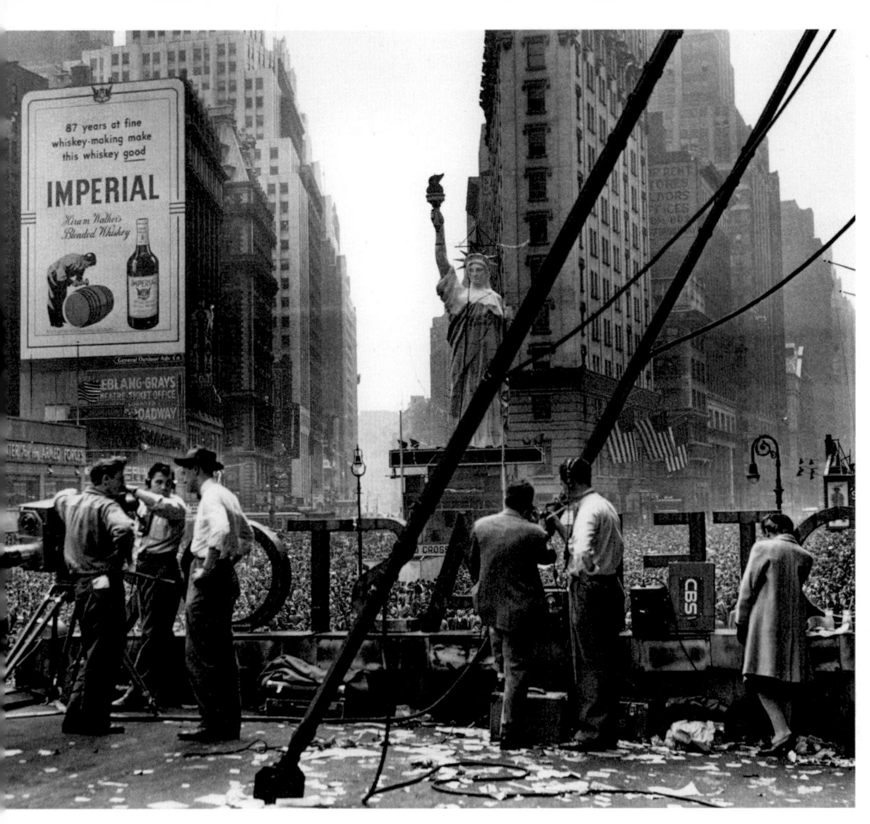
87 years at fine
whiskey-making make
this whiskey good
IMPERIAL
Hiram Walker's
Blended Whiskey
General Outdoor Adv. Co.
LEBLANG-GRAYS
THEATRE TICKET OFFICE
BROADWAY
CBS

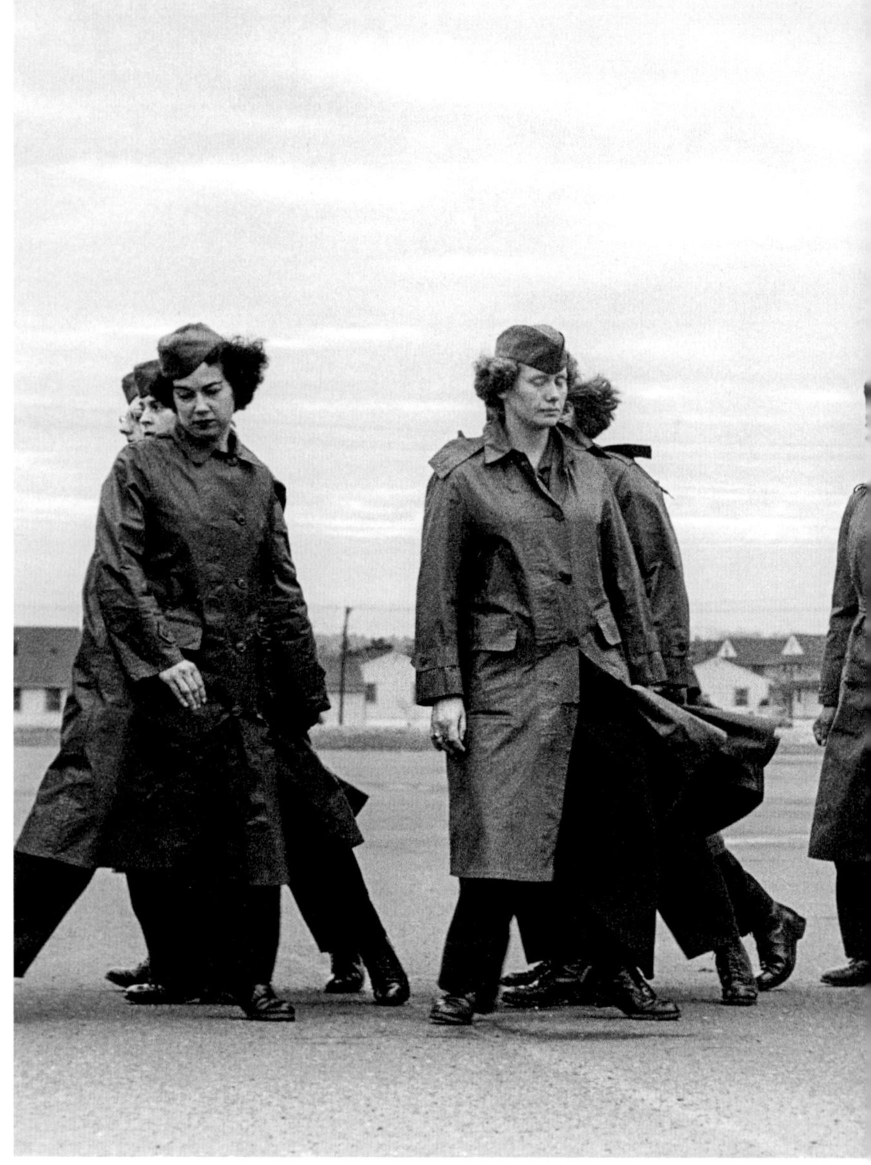

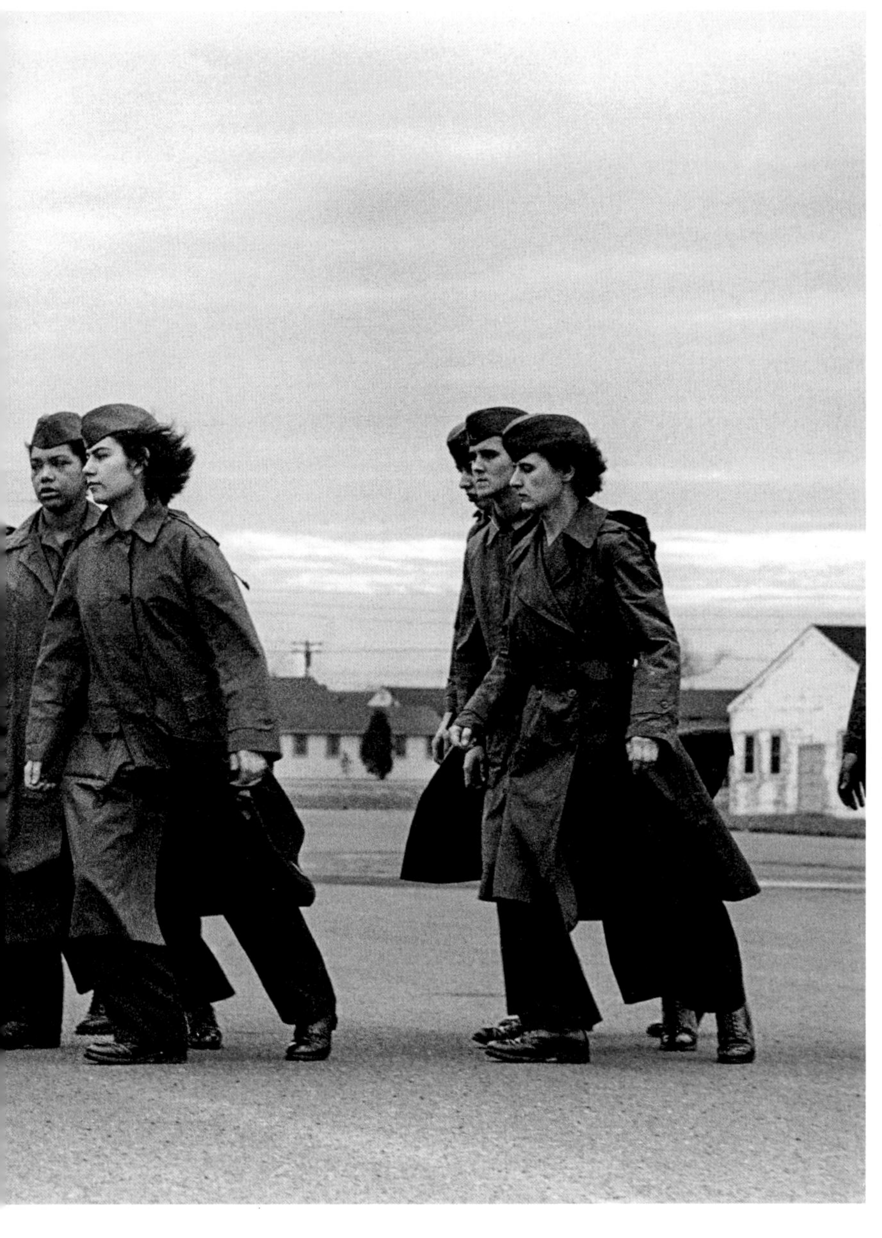

21. Nedick's, New York, 1950.

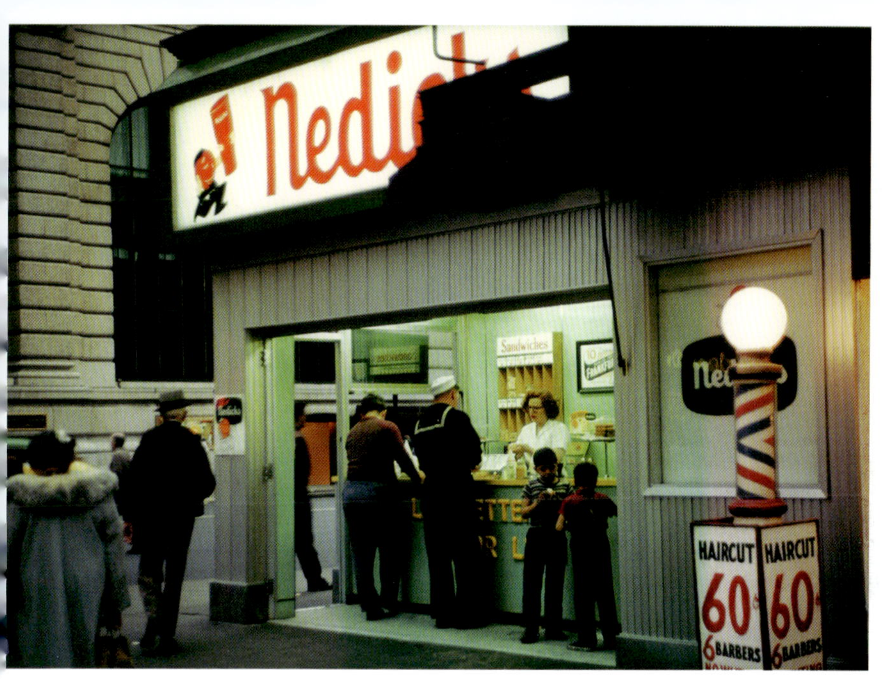

Nedick's
Sandwiches
Nedick's
HAIRCUT
60¢
6 BARBERS
HAIRCUT
60¢
6 BARBERS

22. Sandstorm, West Village, New York, 1949.

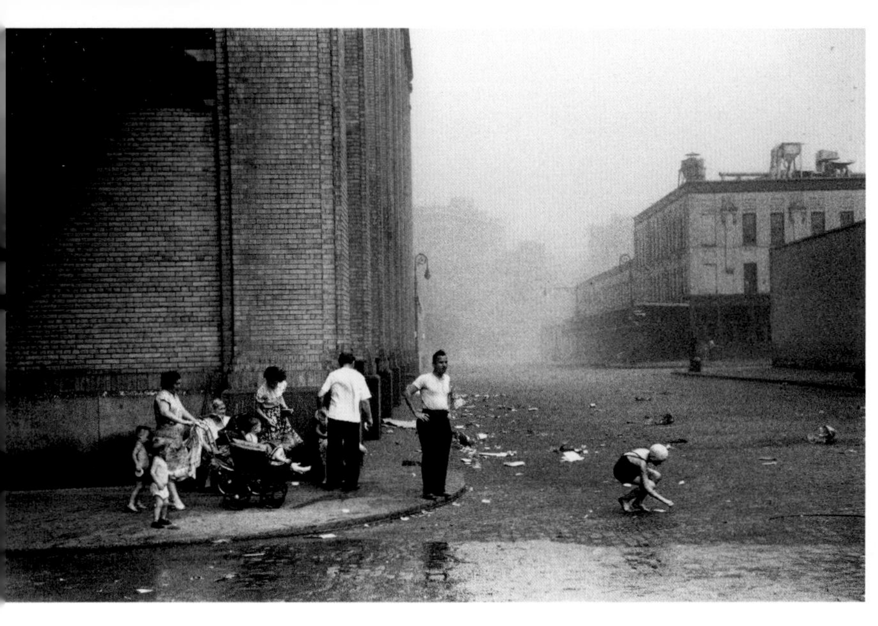

23. Street shower, West Village, New York, 1948.

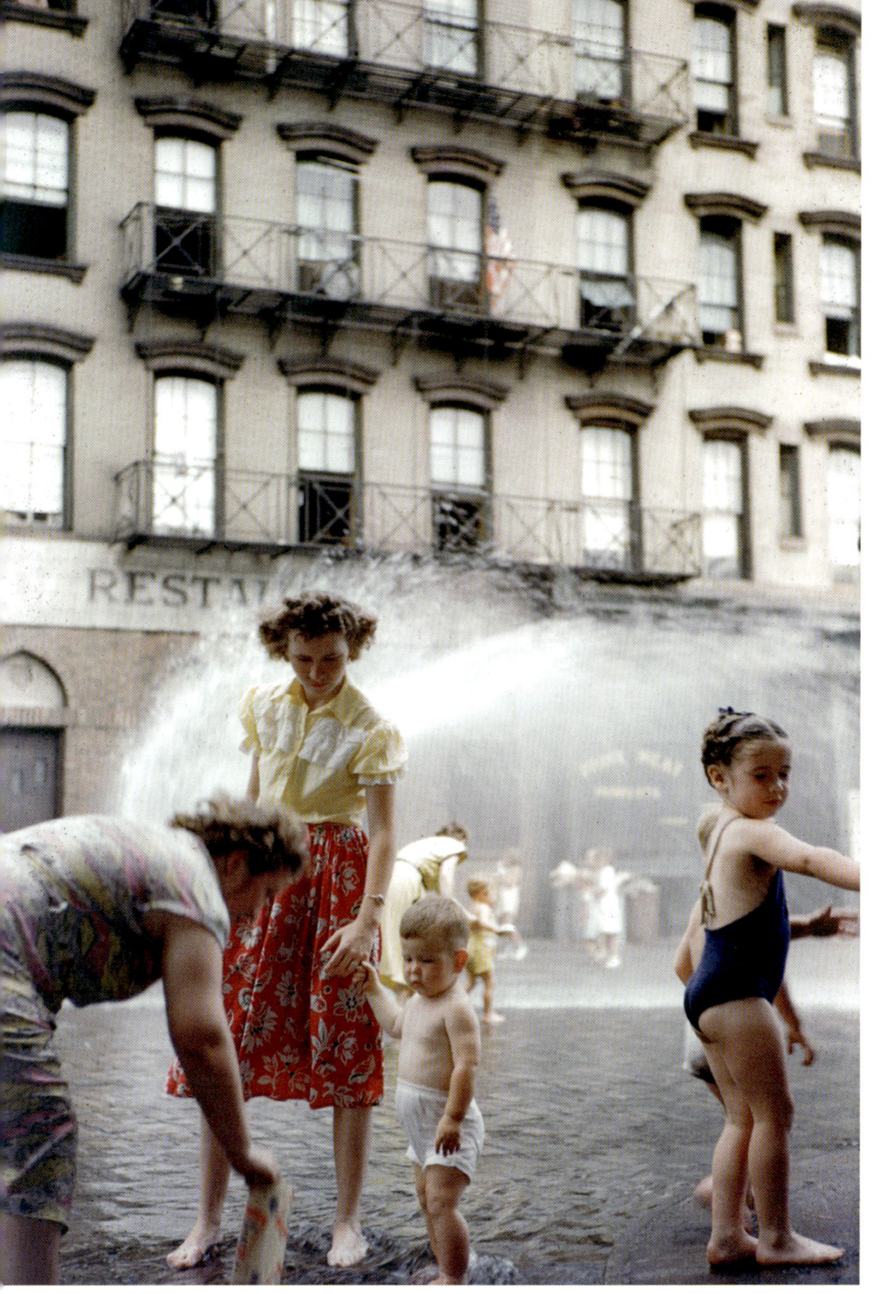

24. Boy jumping into Hudson River,
Gansevoort Pier, New York, 1948.

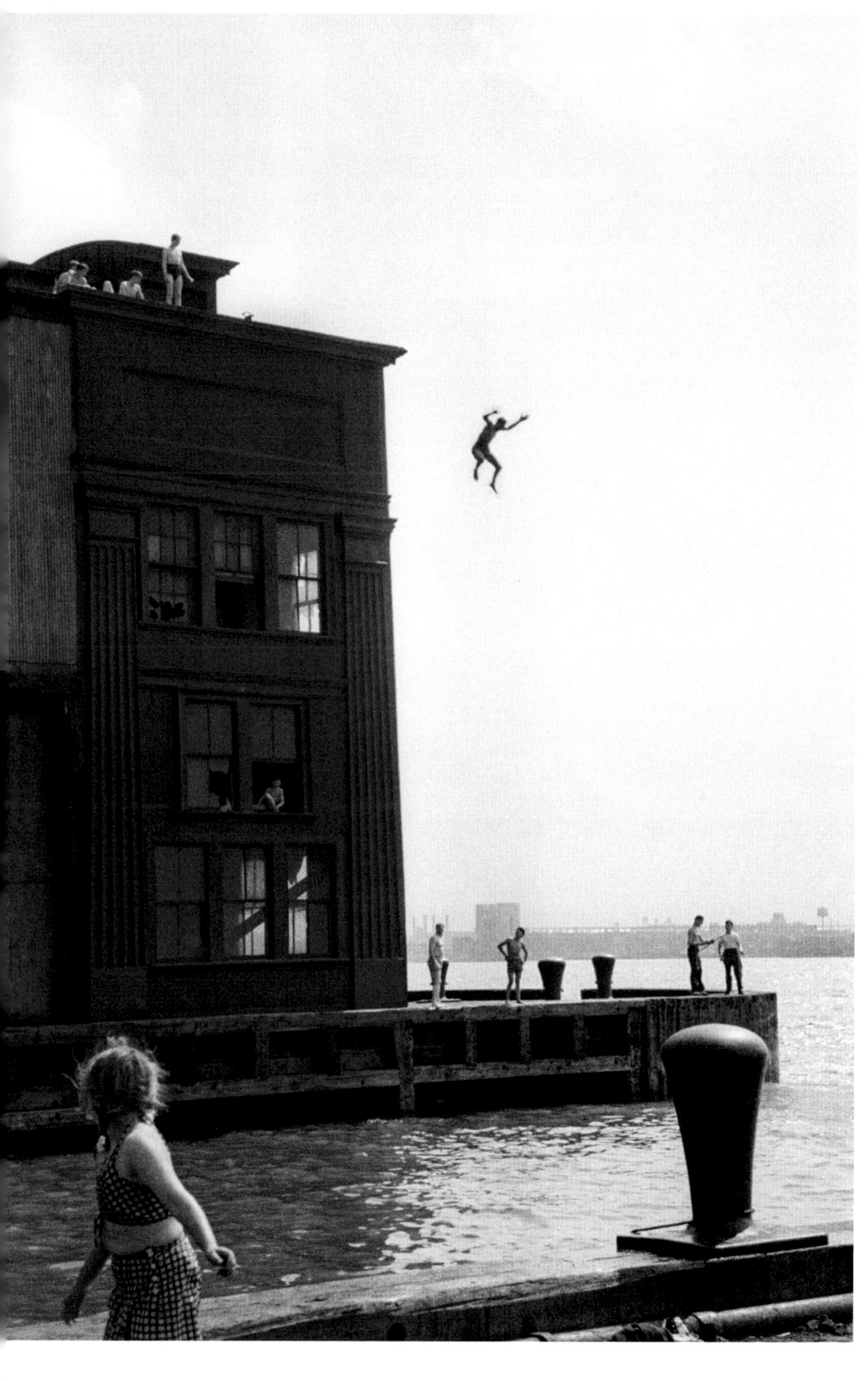

25. Boys on logs, Gansevoort Pier, New York, 1948.

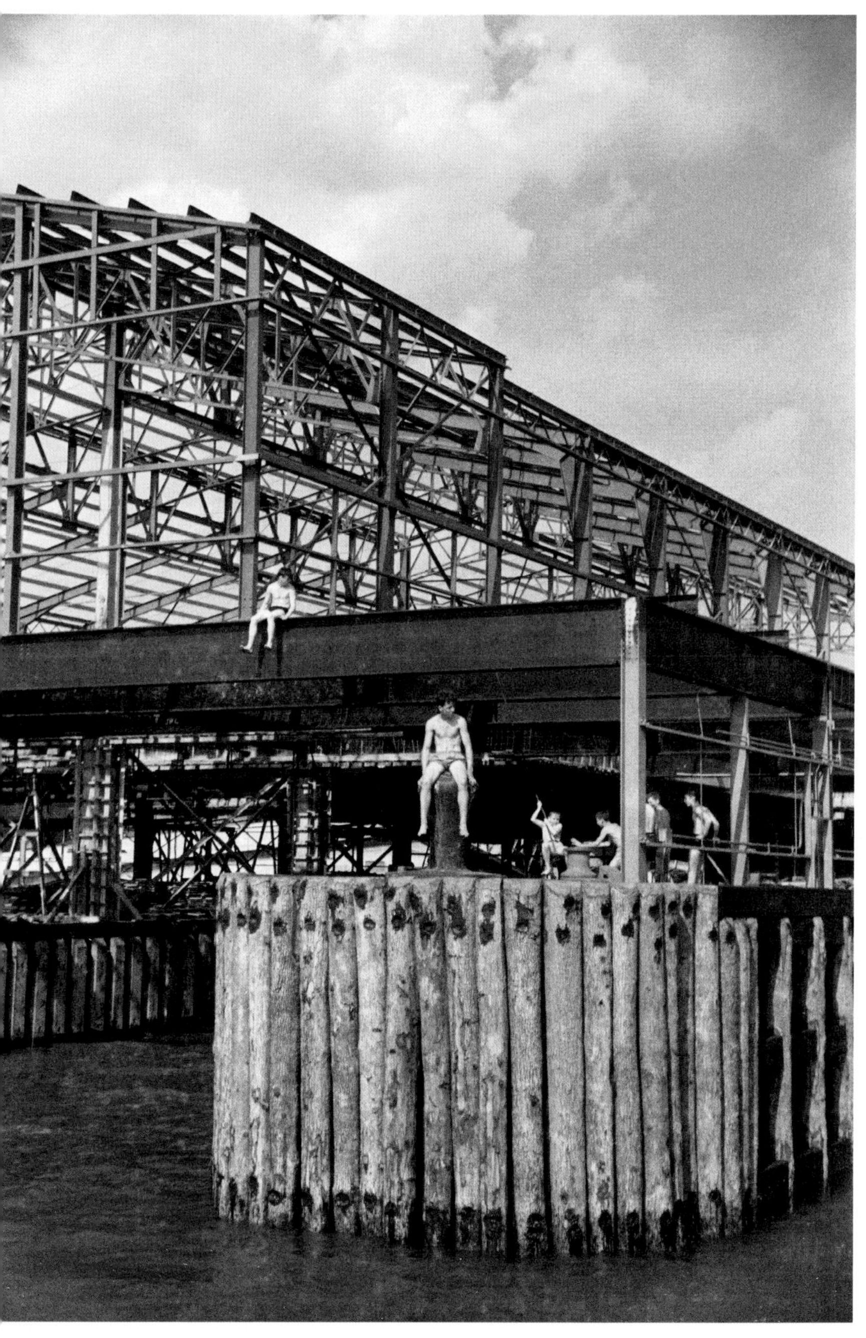

26. Couple on the beach, Coney Island, New York, 1949.

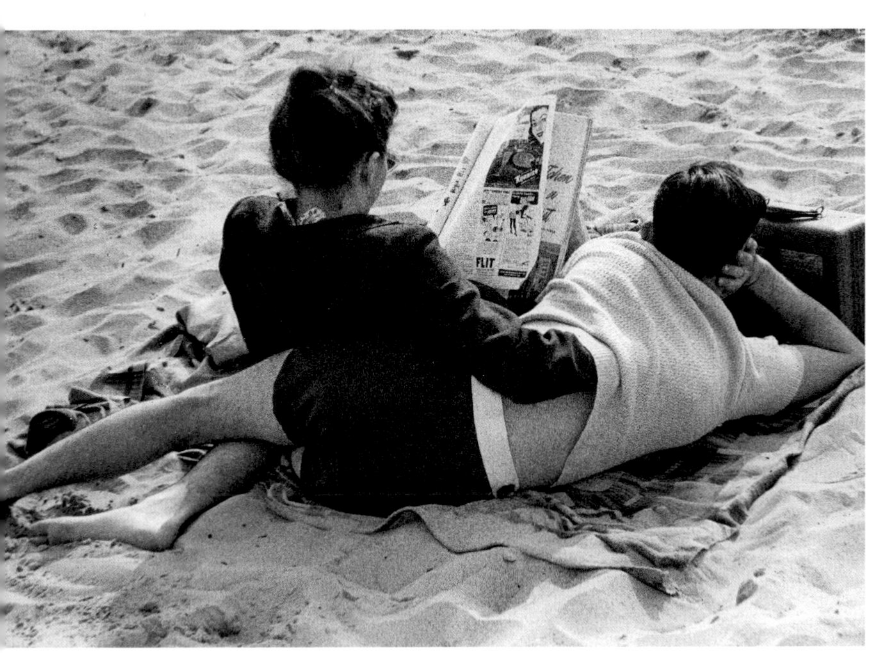
FLIT

27. People taking photos, World's Fair, New York, 1964.

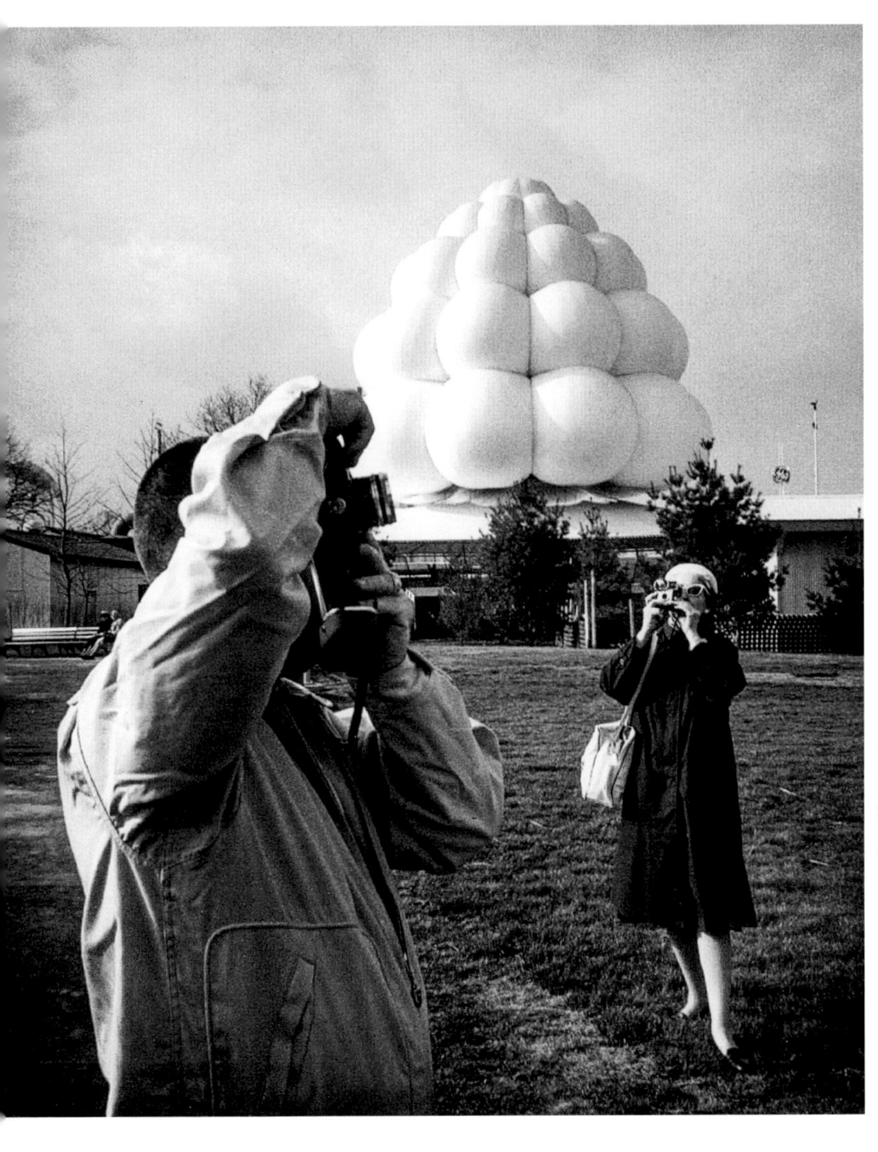

28. Museum, boy looking at statue,
location unknown, undated.

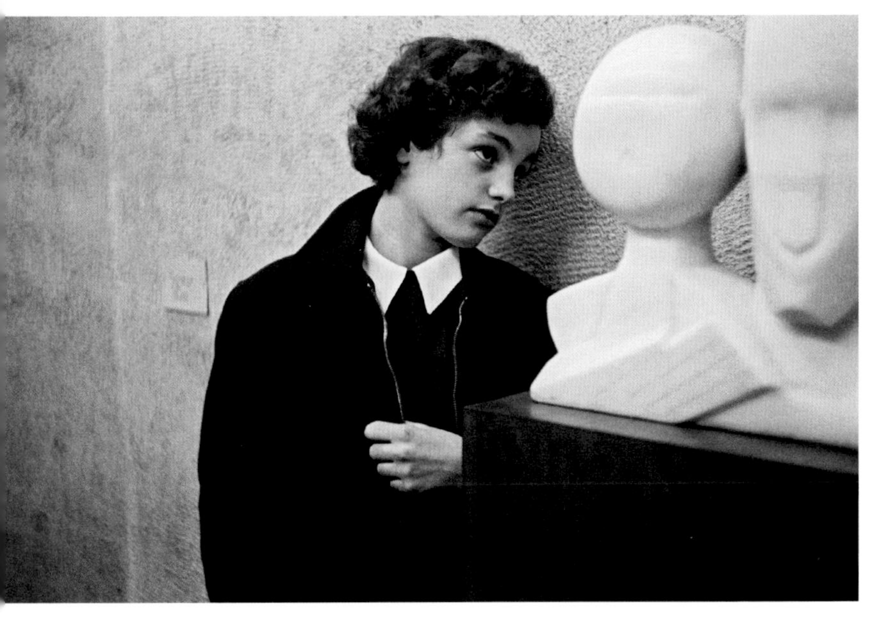

29. 'Jinx staring at a statue', Florence,
from the series *American Girl in Italy*, 1951.

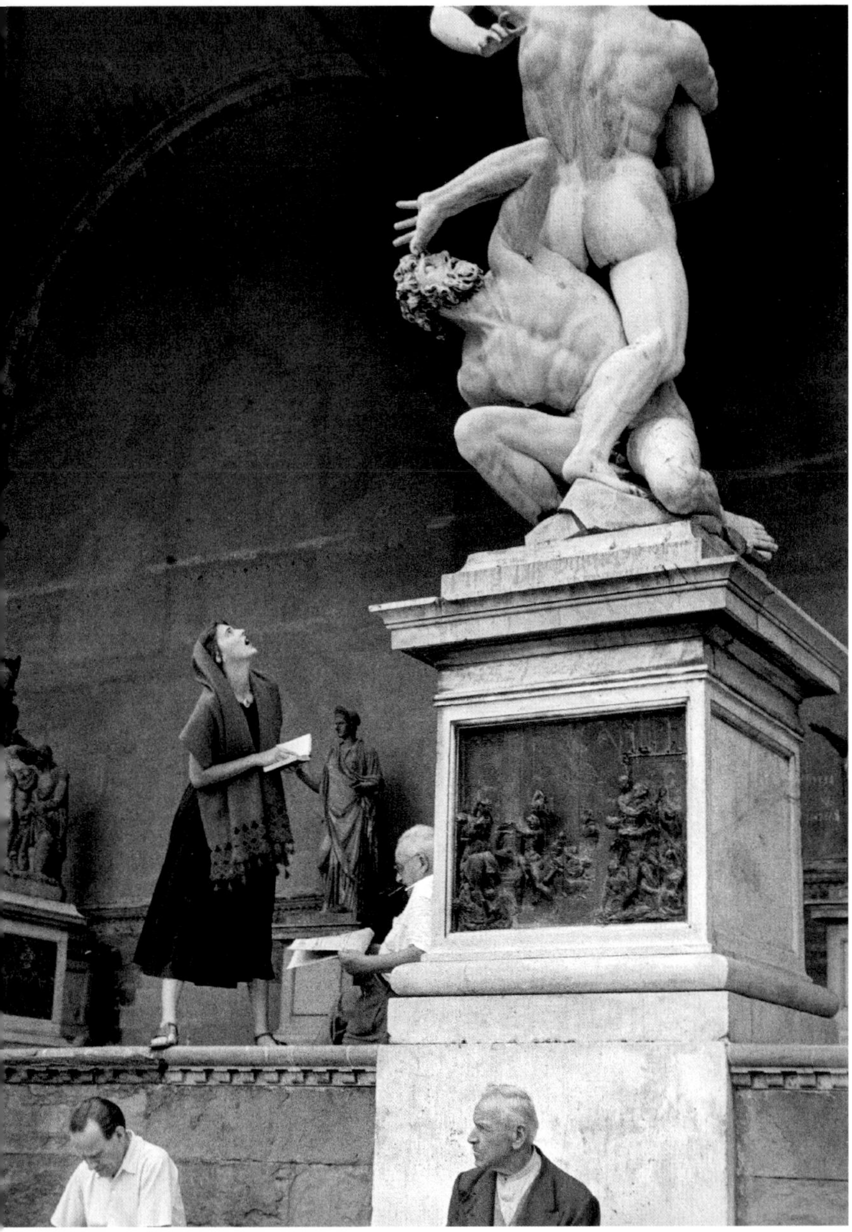

30. Couple with statue, Rome, 1951.

Overleaf:
31. 'Jinx and cars', Florence, from
the series *American Girl in Italy*, 1951.

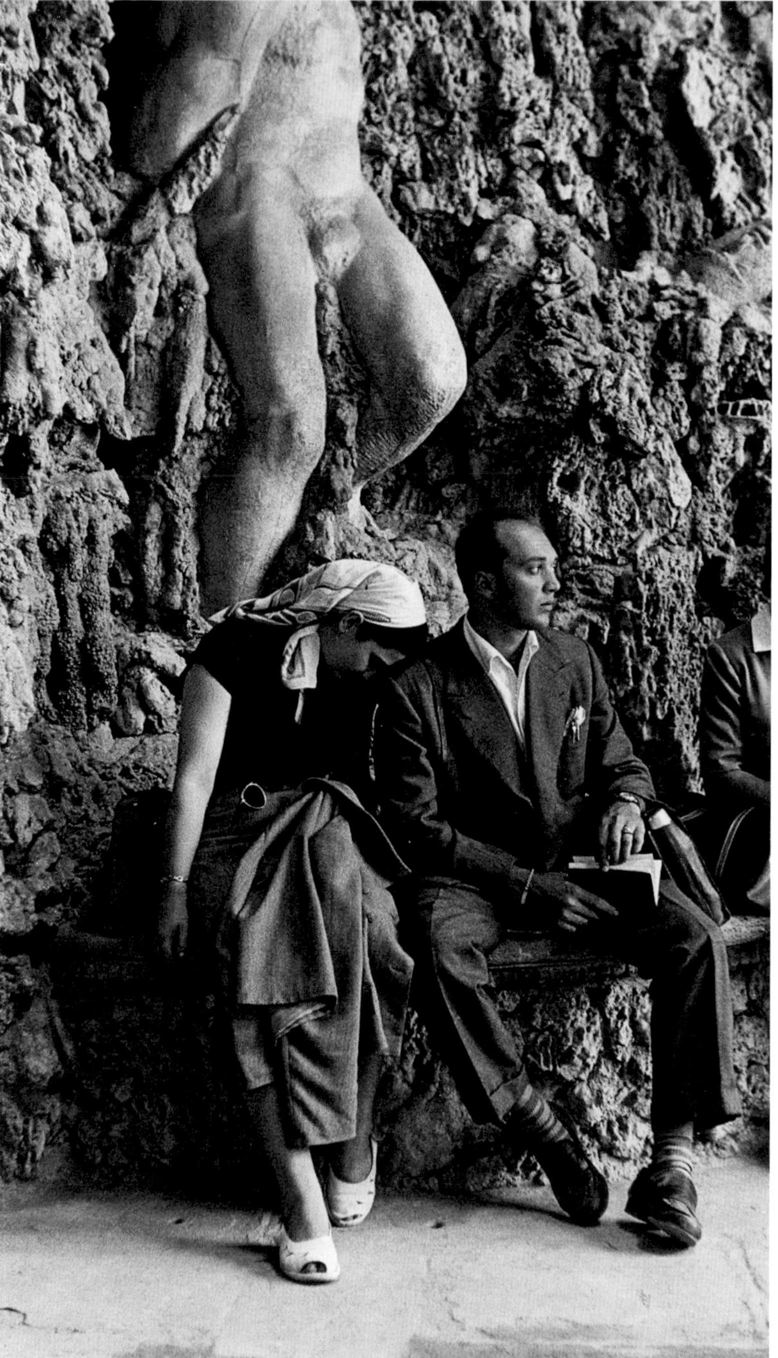

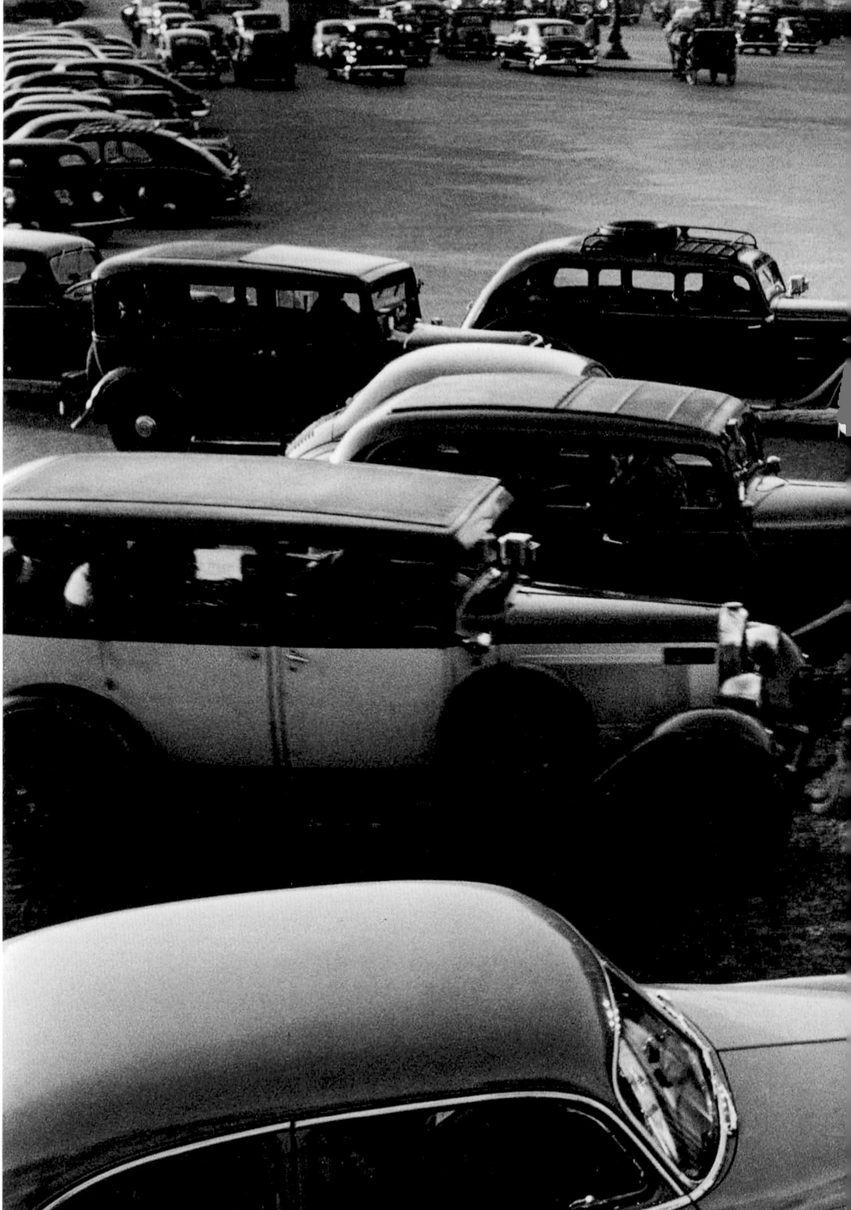

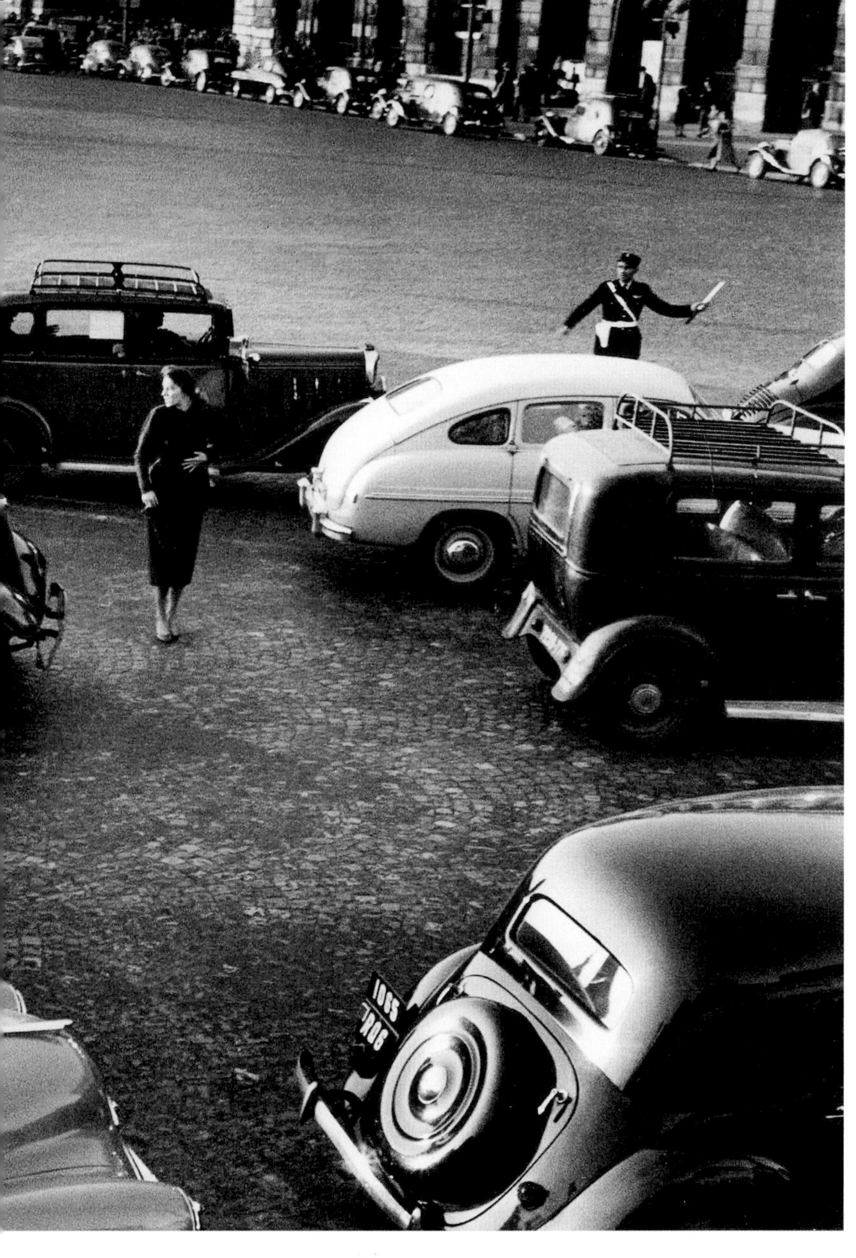

32. 'American Girl in Italy', Florence,
from the series *American Girl in Italy*, 1951.

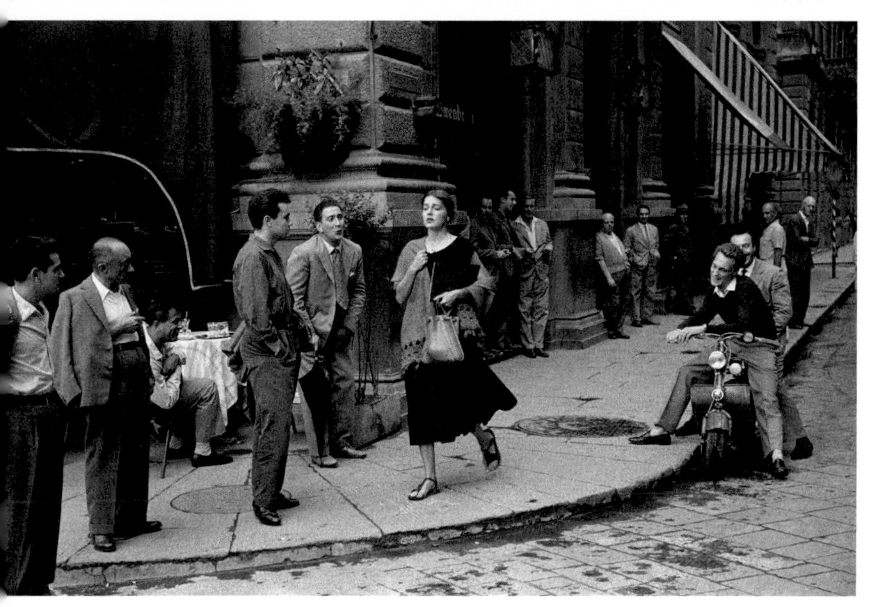

33. 'Jinx and Justin in an MG', Florence,
from the series *American Girl in Italy*, 1951.

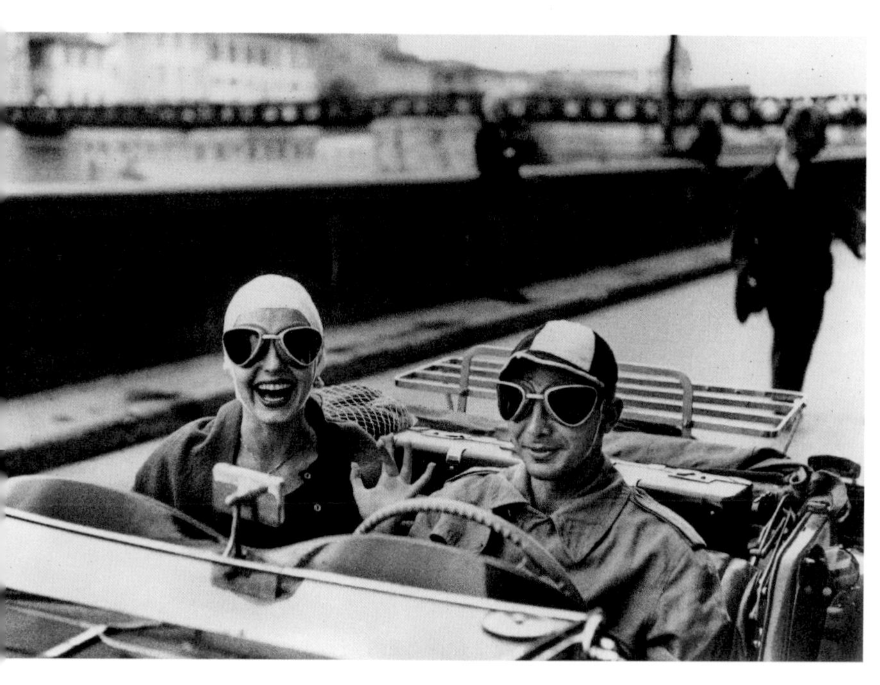

34. 'Jinx with cop', Florence, from
the series *American Girl in Italy*, 1951.

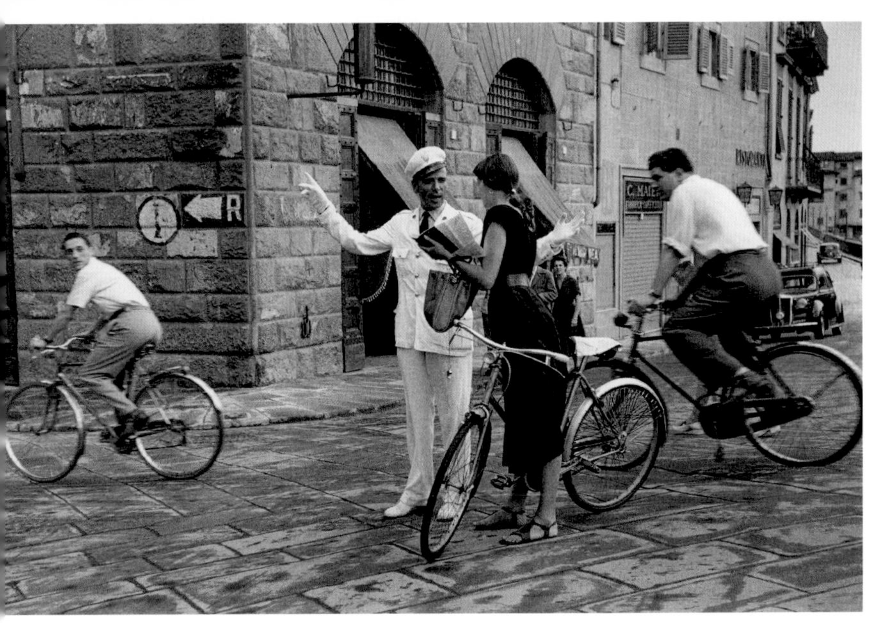
R

\35. Vittorio De Sica, Italy, 1951.

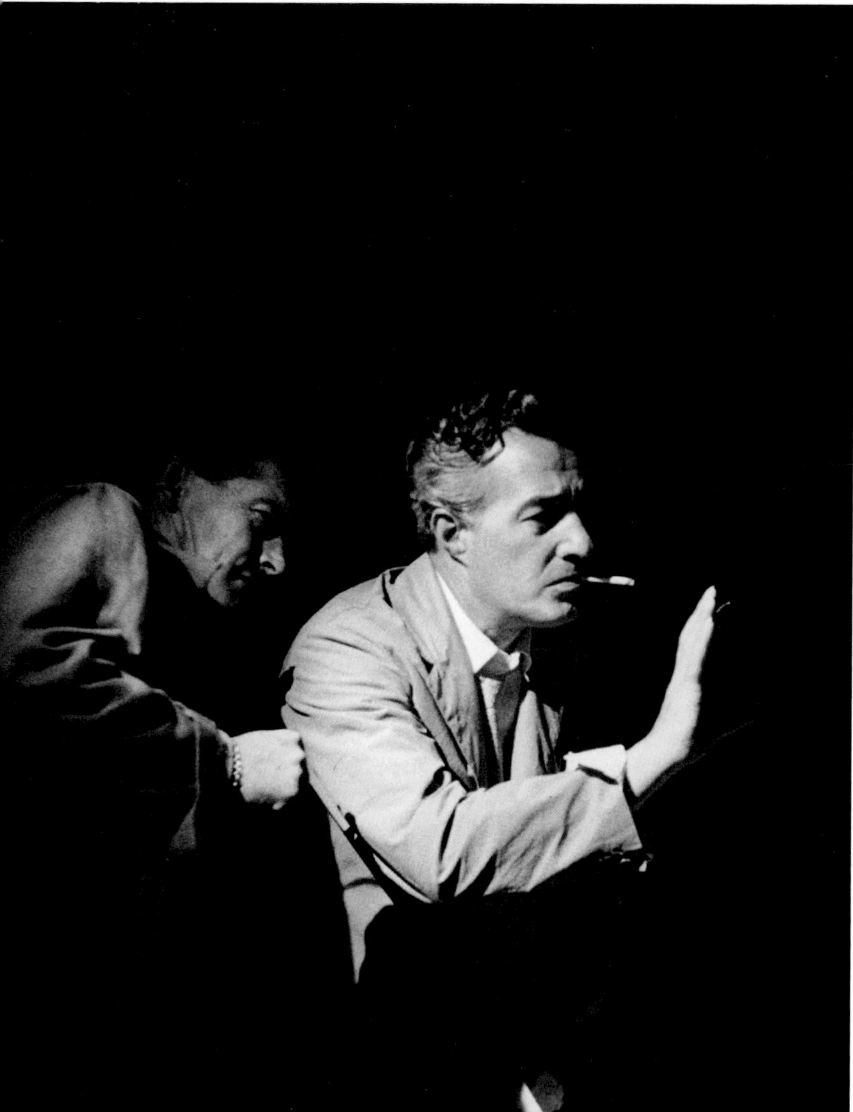

36. Desi Arnaz and Karl Freund on the set
of *I Love Lucy*, Hollywood, Los Angeles, 1952.

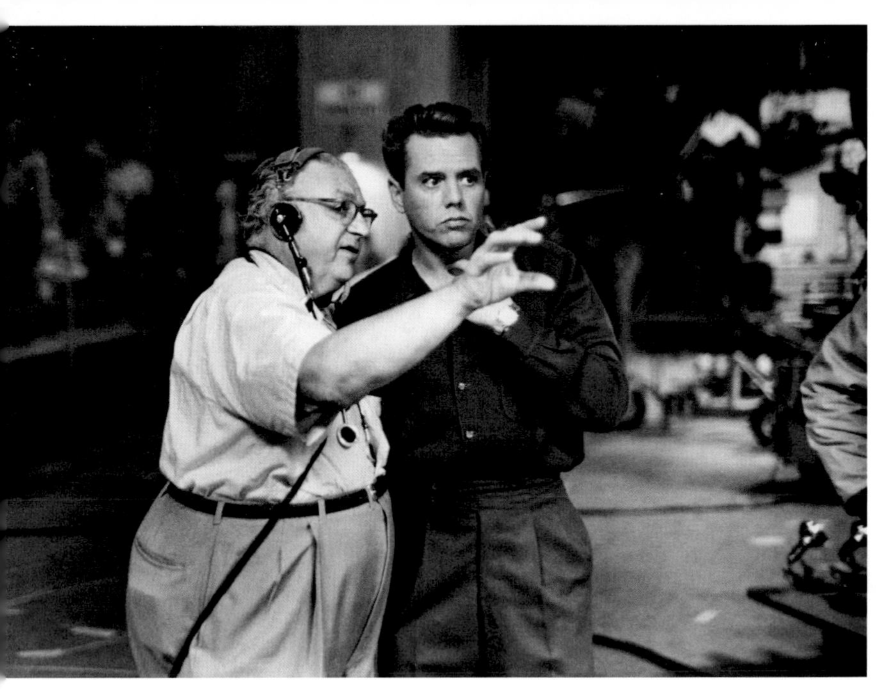

37. Tennessee Williams on the set of
A Streetcar Named Desire, New York, 1950.

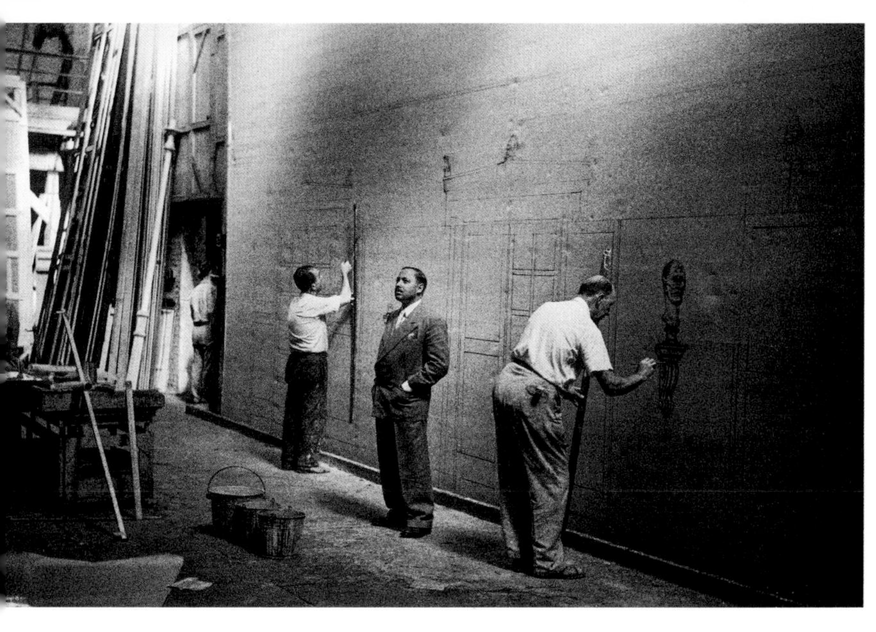

38. Lauren Bacall in a hotel room, New York, 1950.

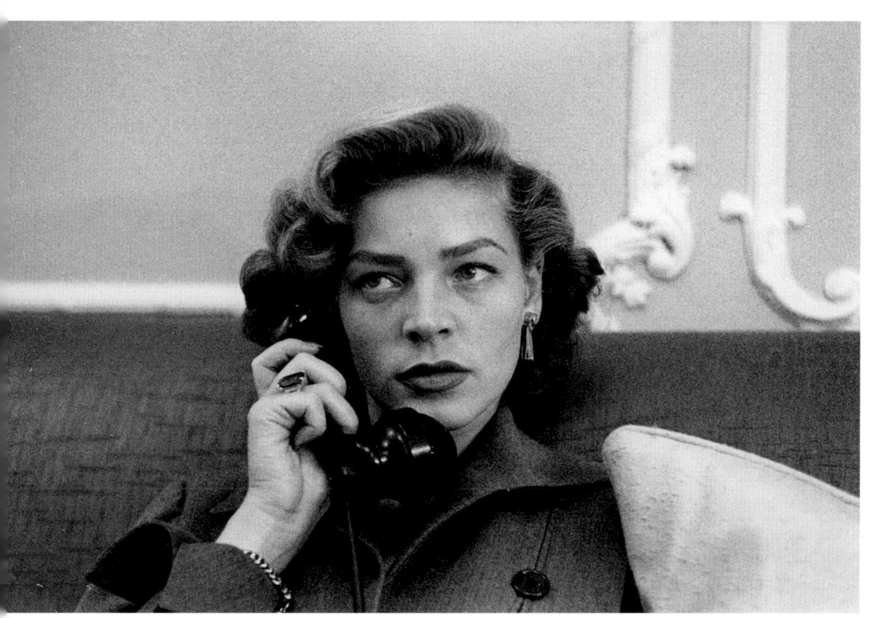

39. Albert Einstein at Princeton luncheon, New Jersey, 1955.

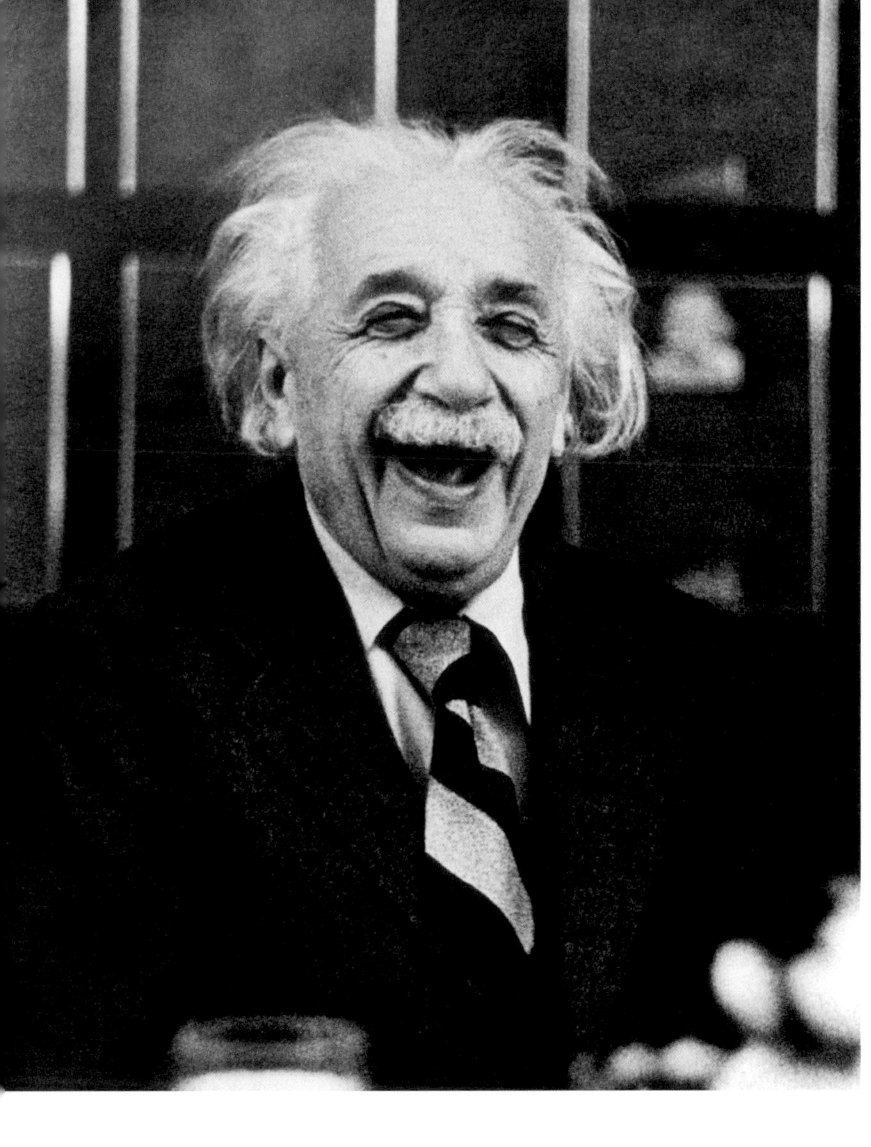

40. Robert Capa in a café, Paris, 1951.

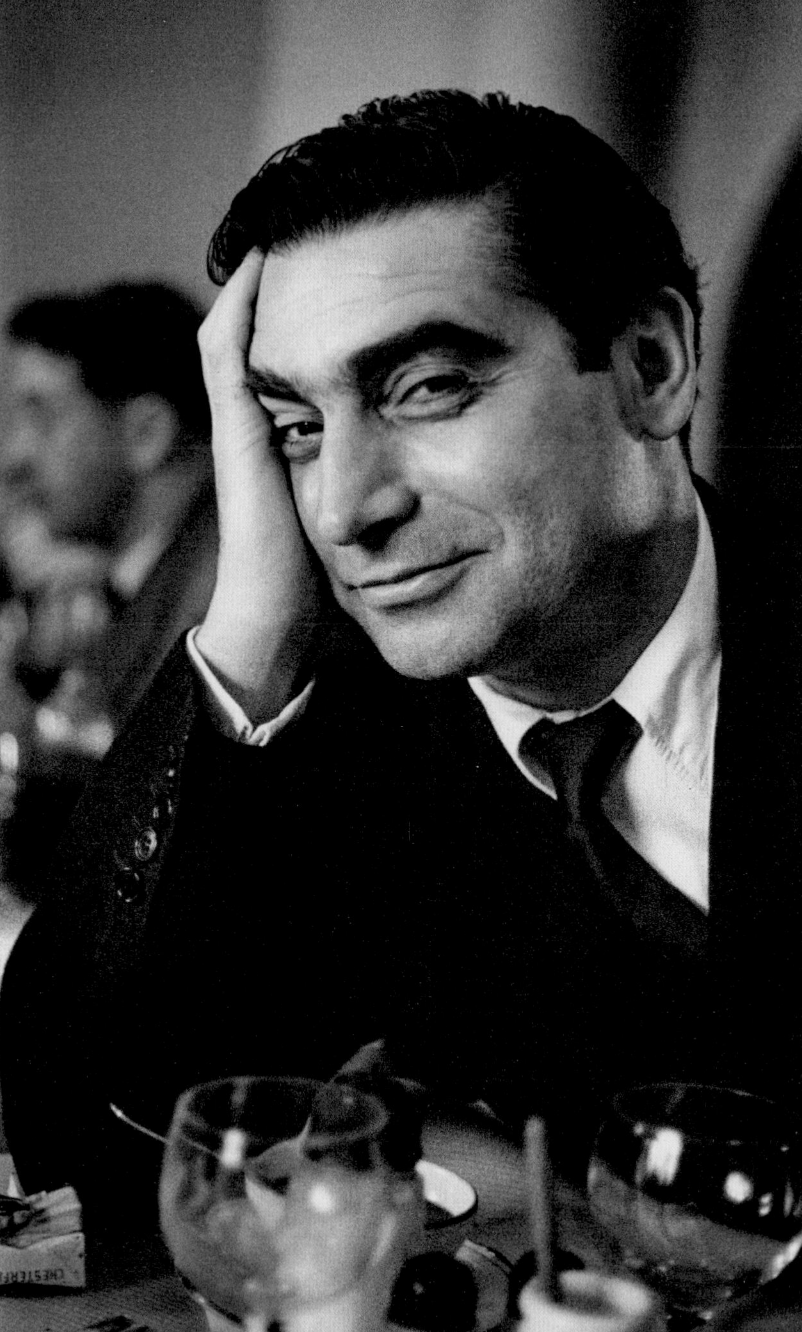

41. 'Waiting for a train', New York,
from the series *Penn Station*, 1948.

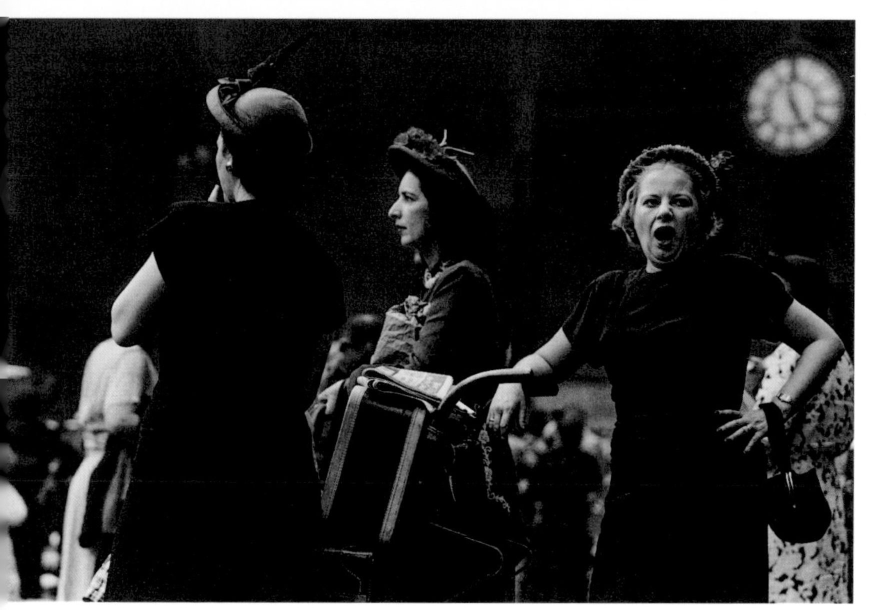

42. 'Little girl with photographers', New York,
from the series *Penn Station*, 1947.

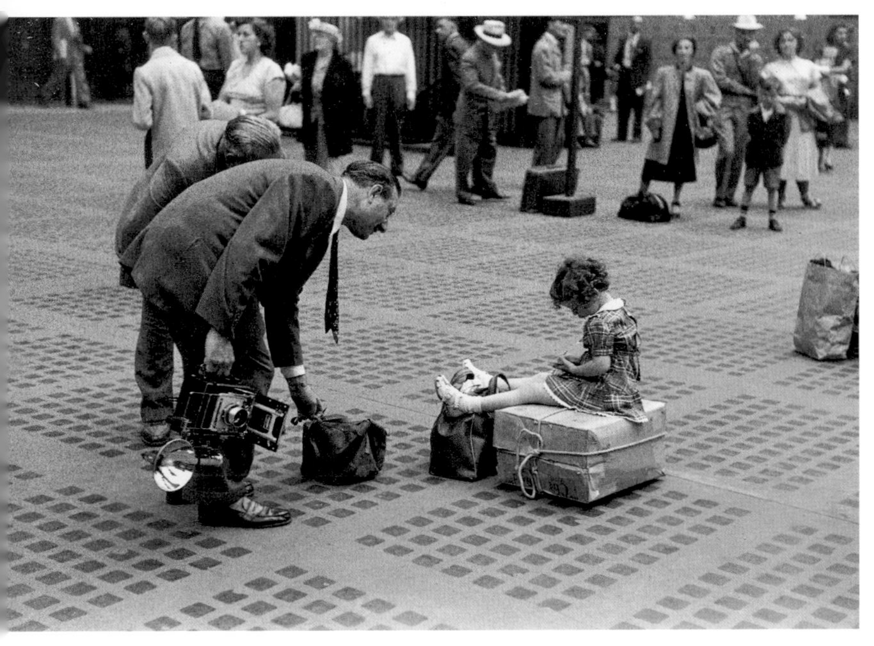

43. Tired little boy after circus, New York, 1949.

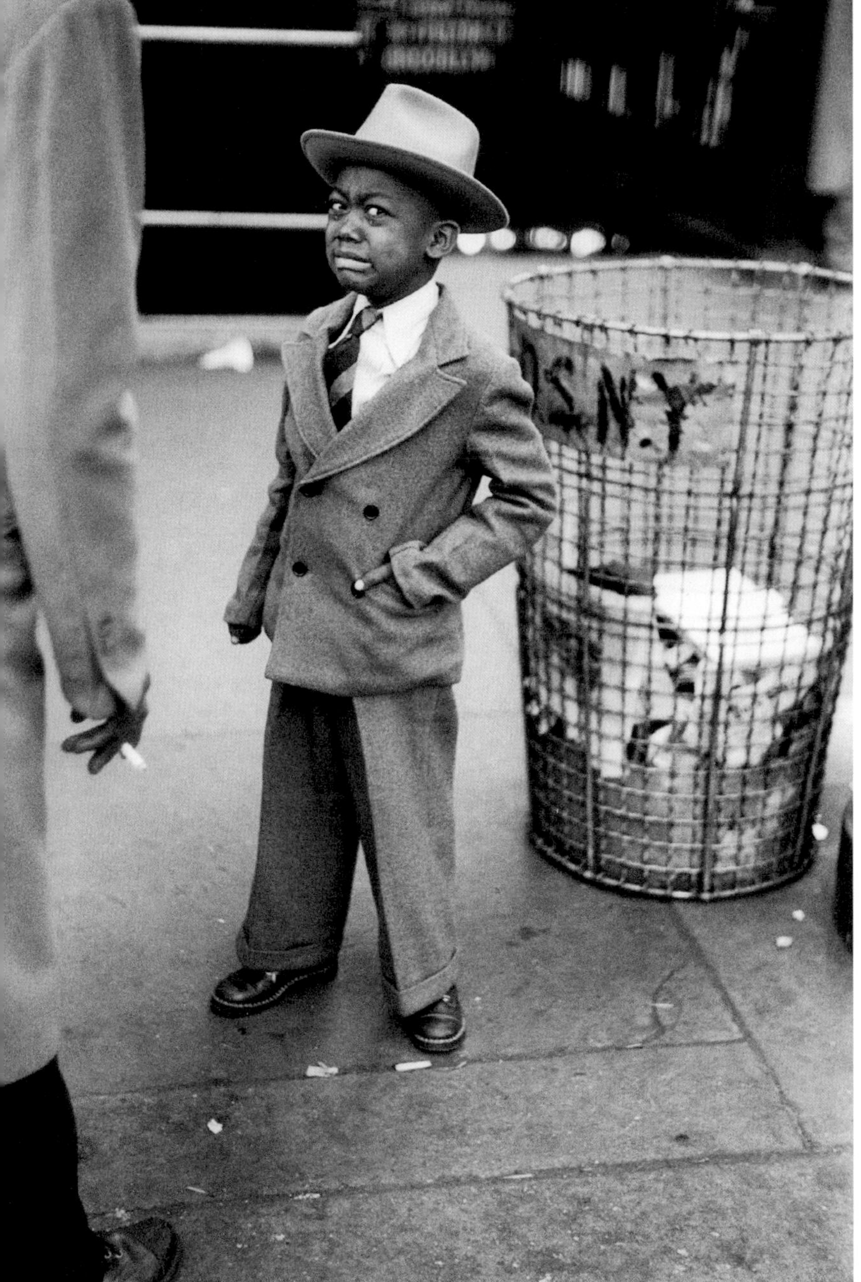

44. Two American tourists, Rome, 1951.

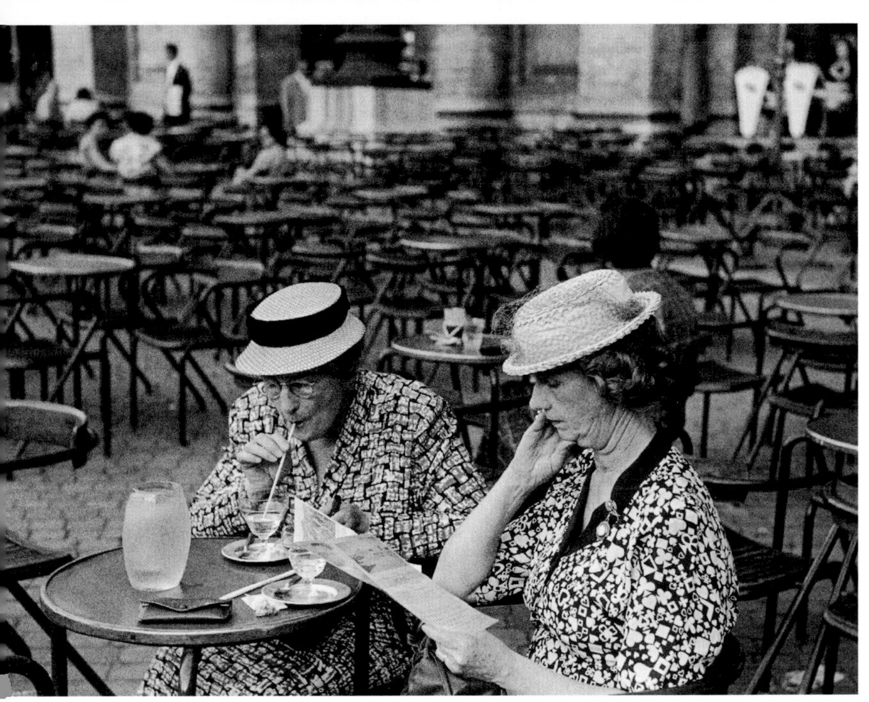

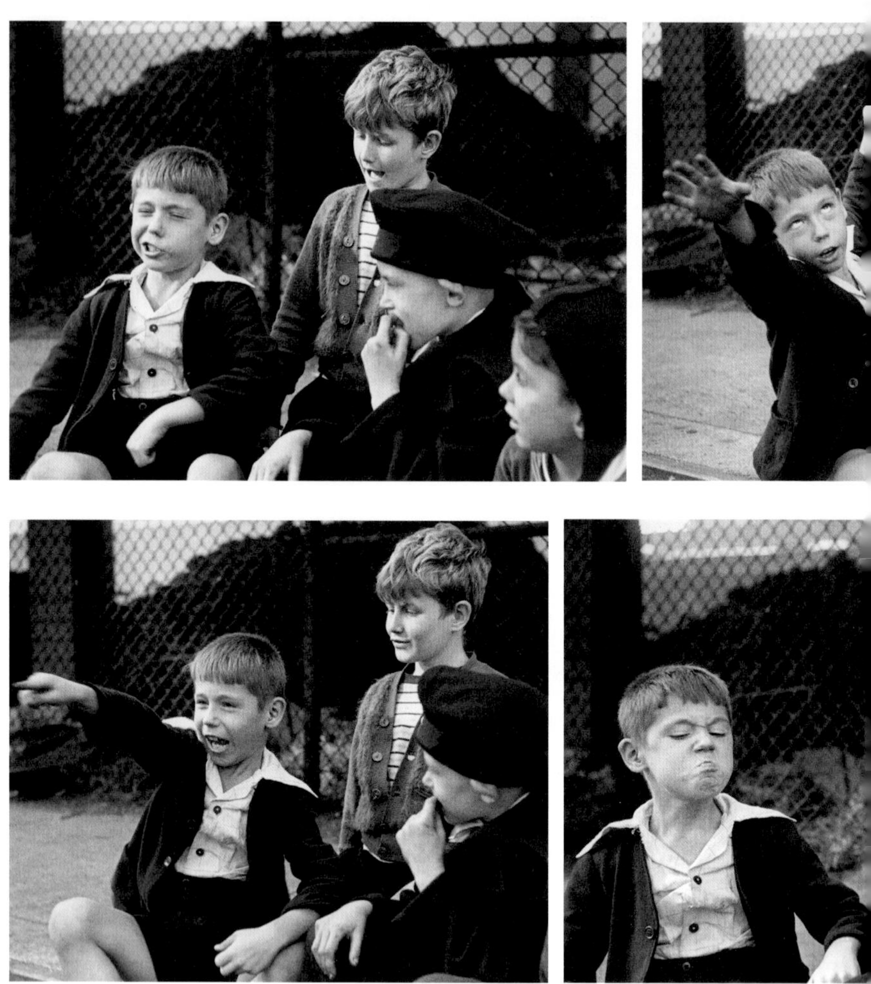

45–50. The series *Jimmy Tells a Story*,
West Village, New York, 1947.

Overleaf:
51. Marian Anderson and Leonard Bernstein,
Lewisohn Stadium, New York, 1947.

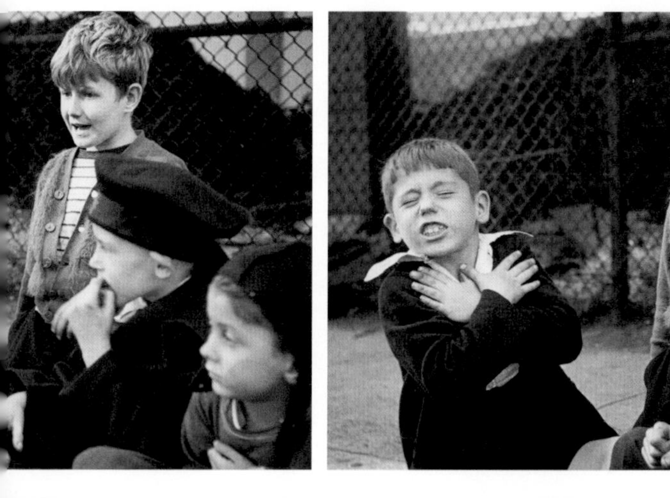

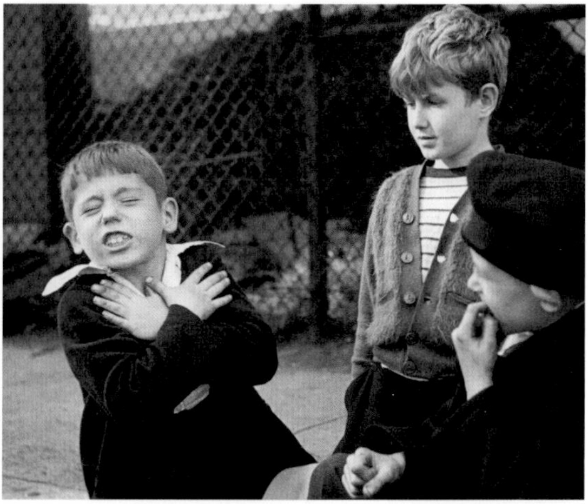

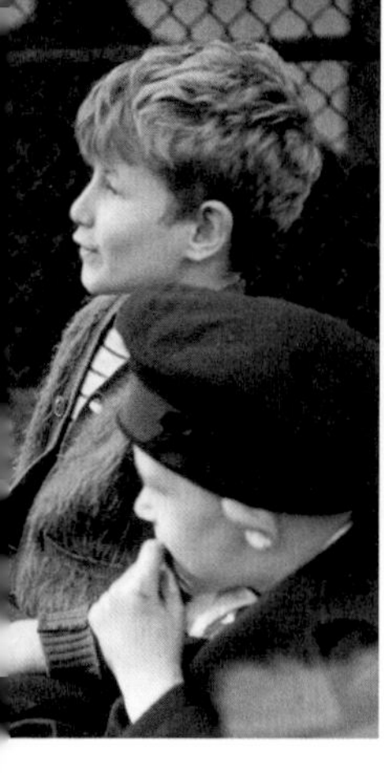

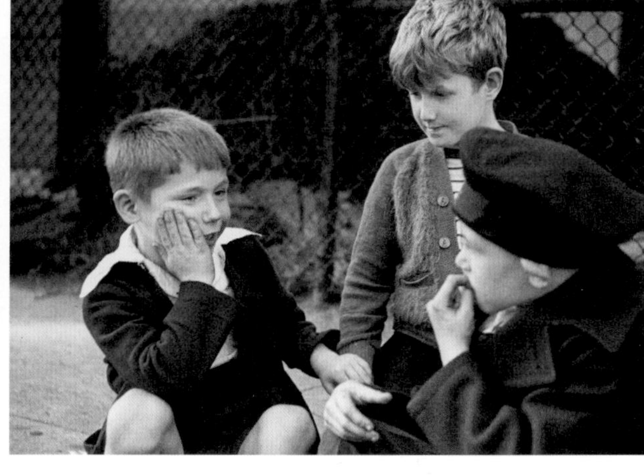

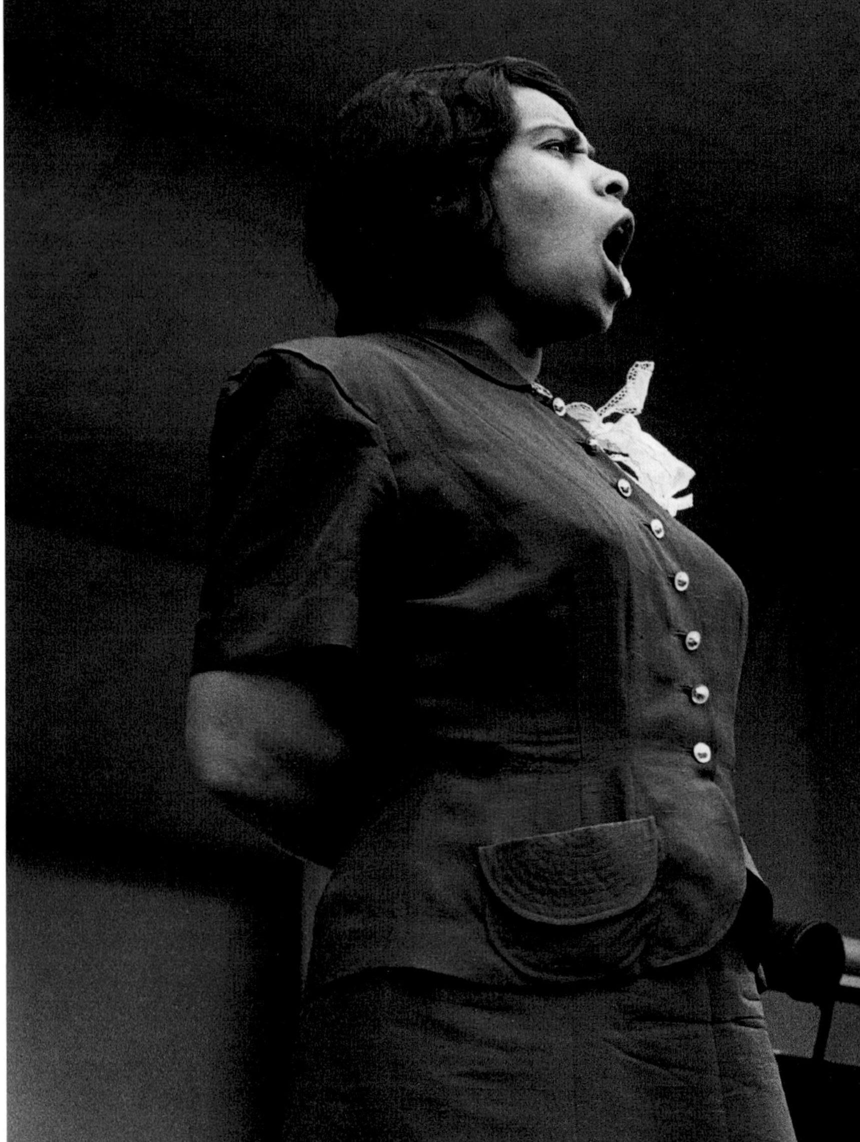

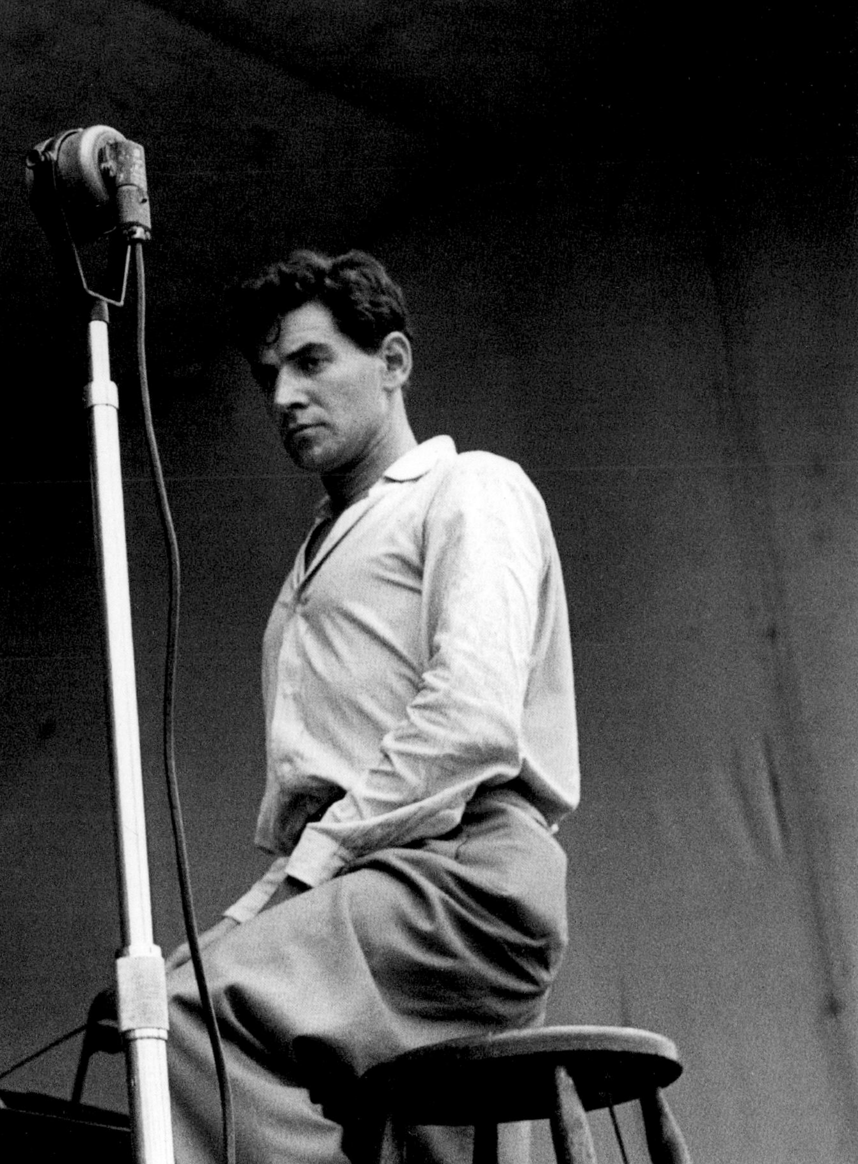

52. Two girls laughing, New York, 1947.

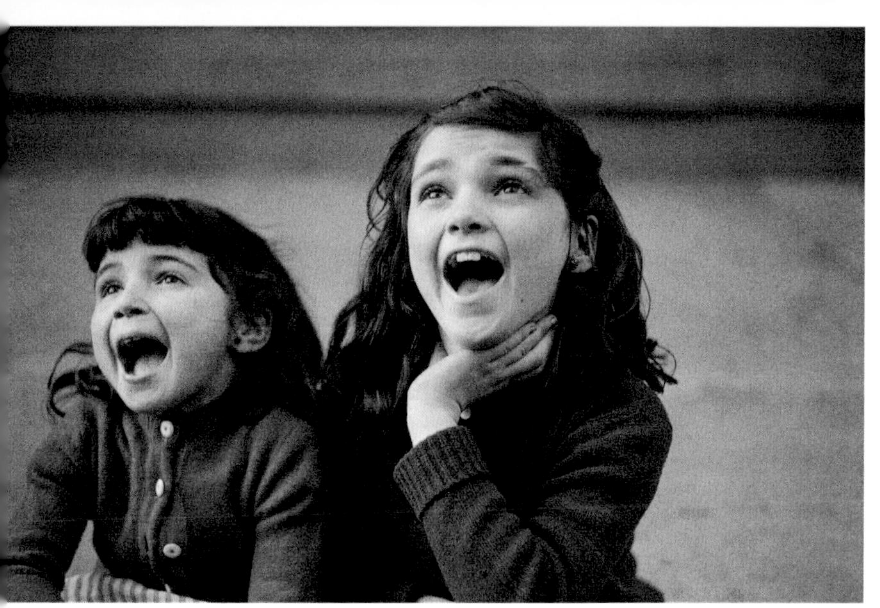

53. Shoeshine boy, New York, 1947.

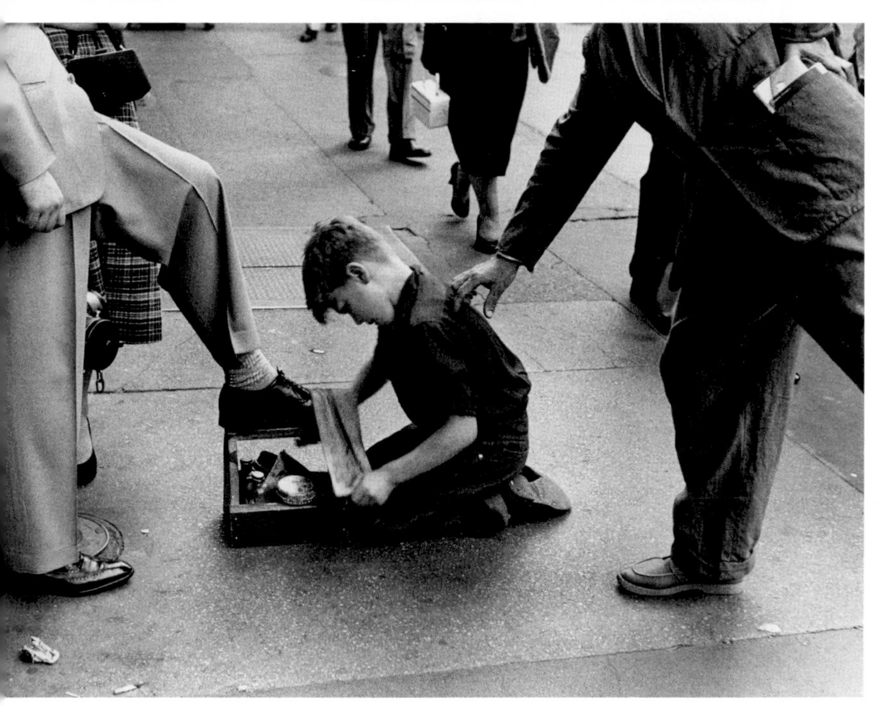

54. Comic book readers, West Village, New York, 1948.

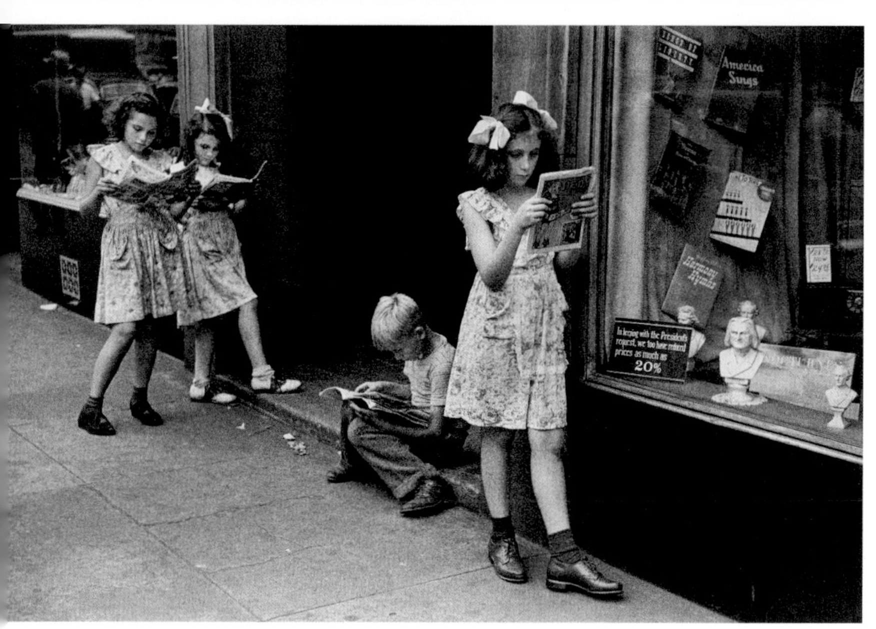

55. 'Big Joke', New York, from the series *Dog Show*, 1949.

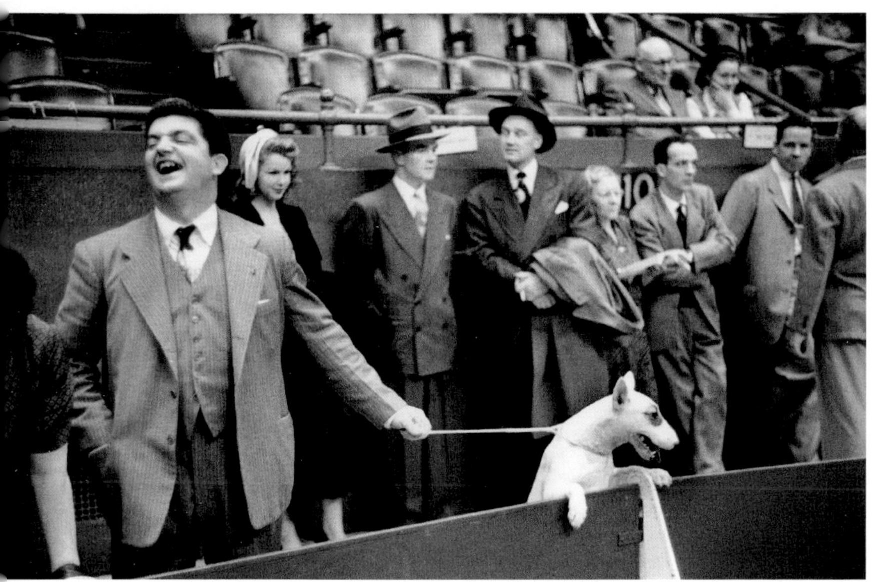

56. Tired driver at Piazza di Spagna, Rome, 1951.

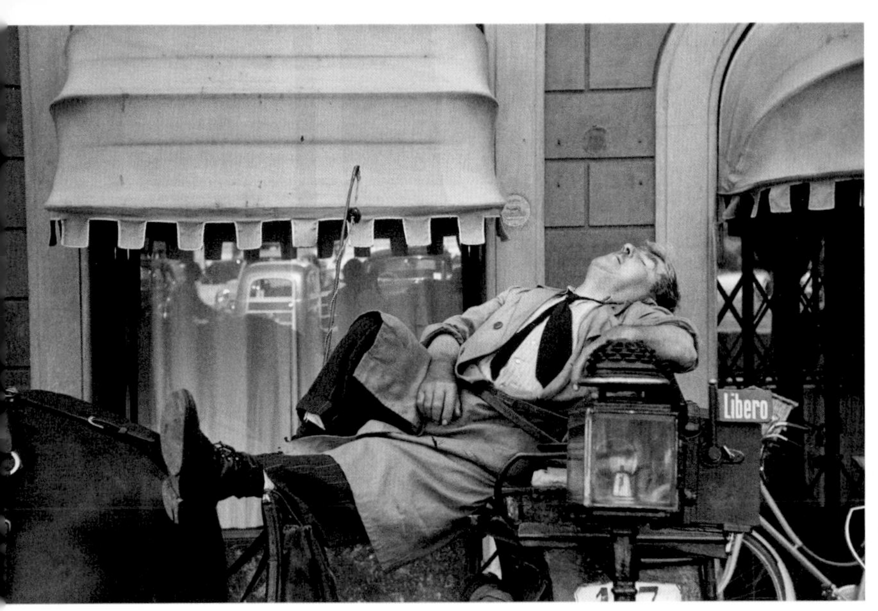
Libero

57. Children at a parade, New York, 1948.

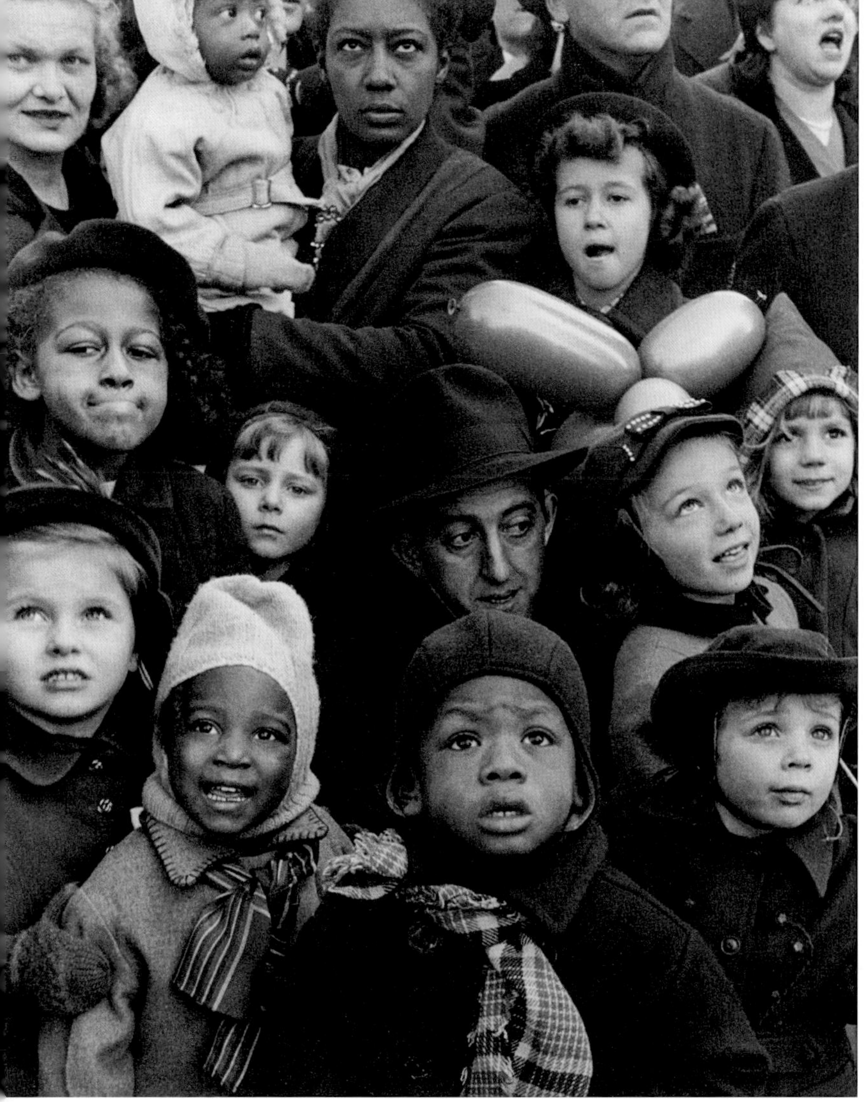

58. Boy with flag, New York, 1949.

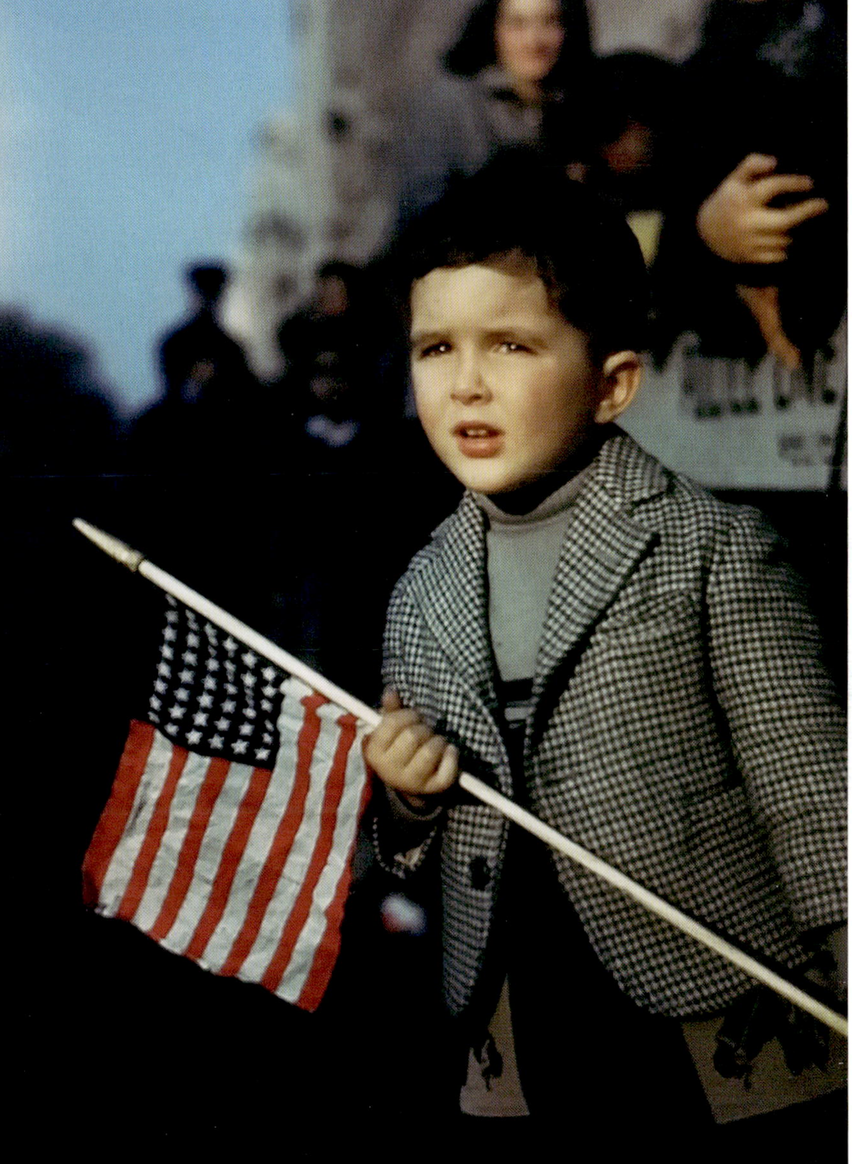

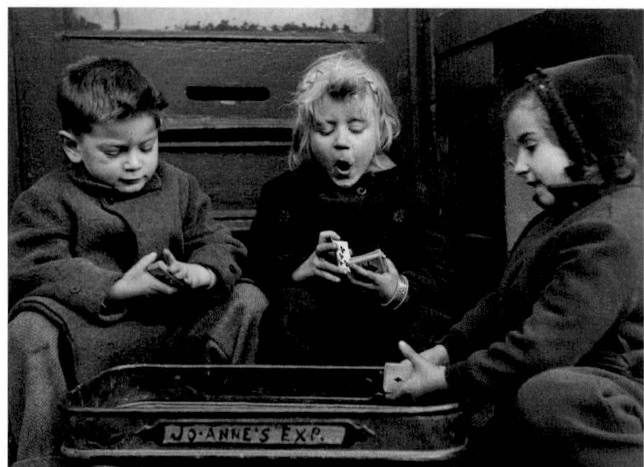
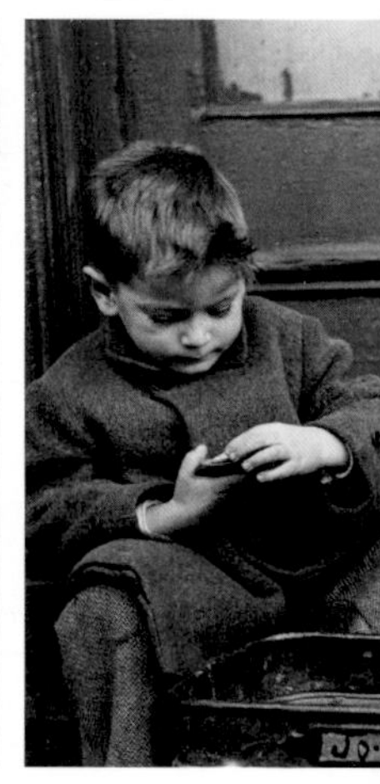
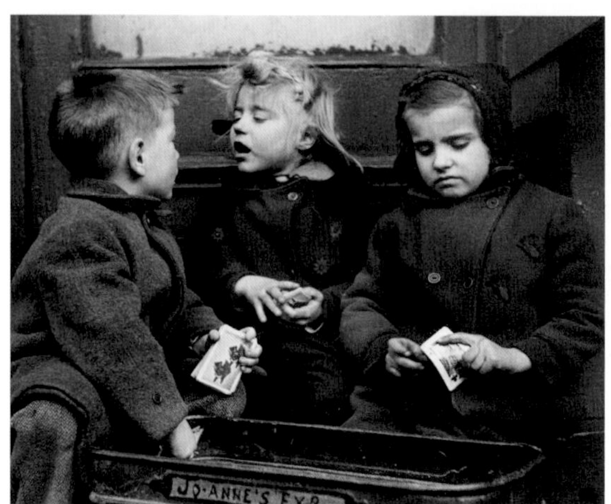
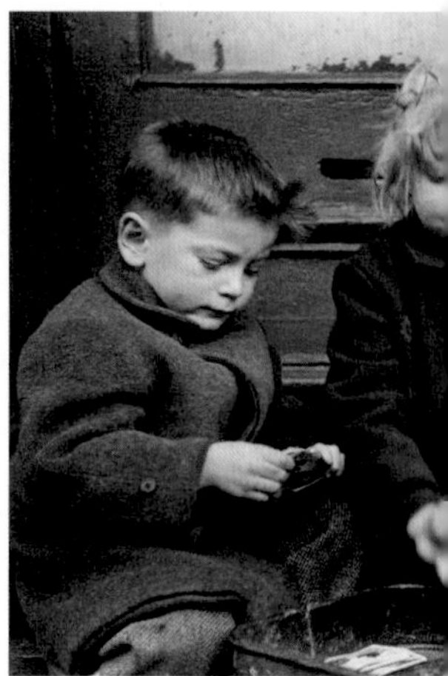

59–64. The series *The Card Players*, New York, 1952.

Overleaf:
65. Coca-Cola, New York, 1950.

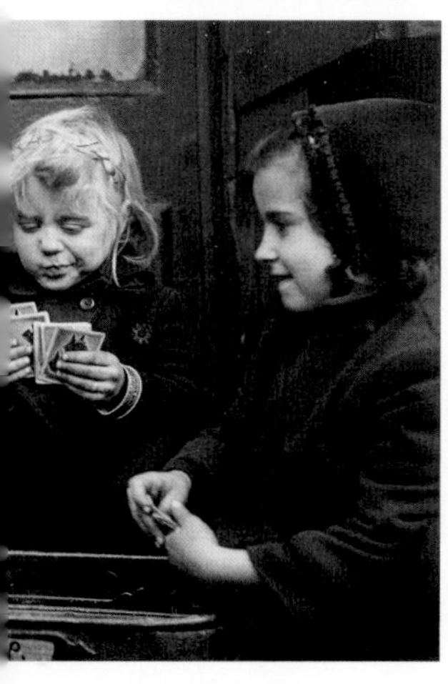
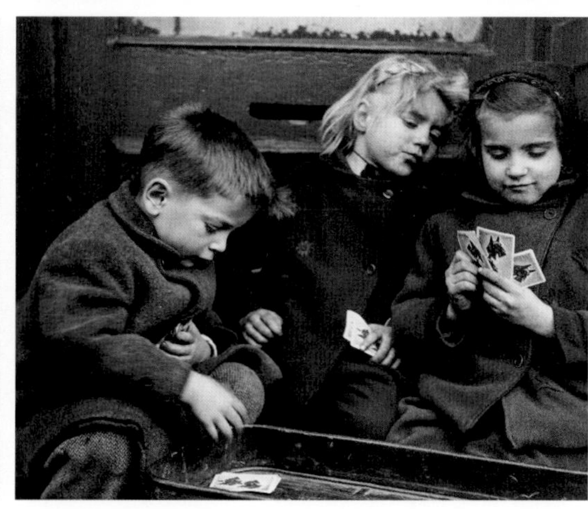
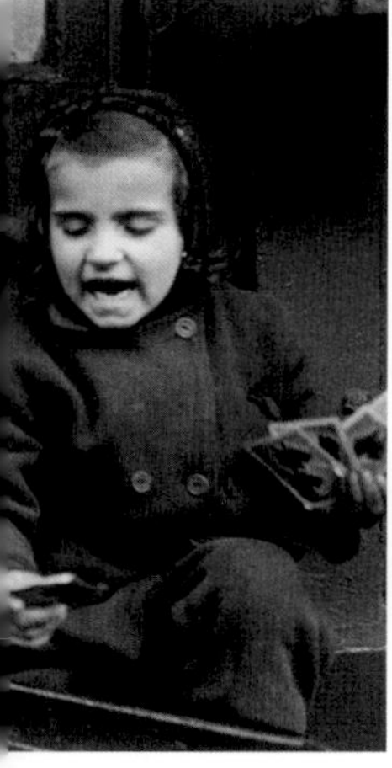
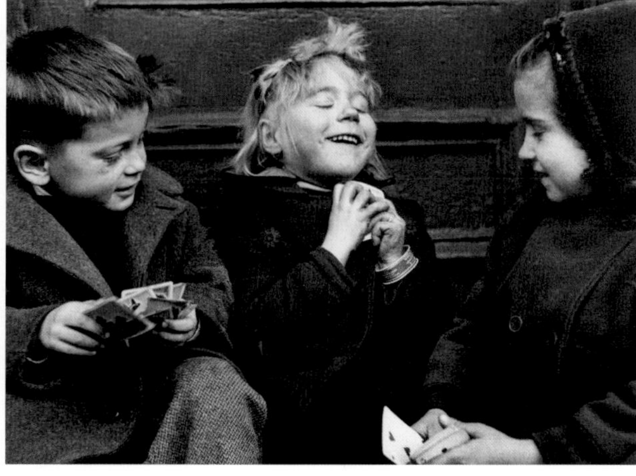

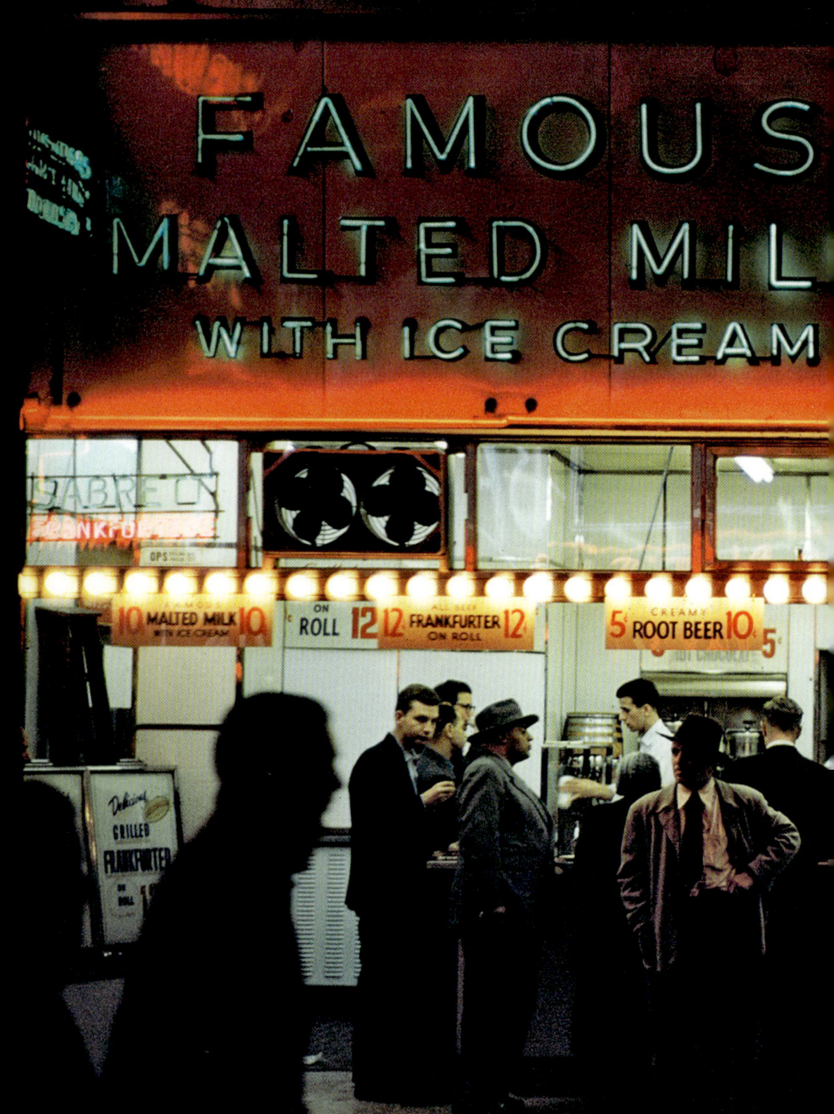

FAMOUS
MALTED MIL
WITH ICE CREAM
FRANKFURTERS
10¢ MALTED MILK 10¢
WITH ICE CREAM
ON ROLL 12¢ 12¢ FRANKFURTER 12¢
ON ROLL
5¢ ROOT BEER 10¢ 5¢
Delicious GRILLED FRANKFURTER ON ROLL

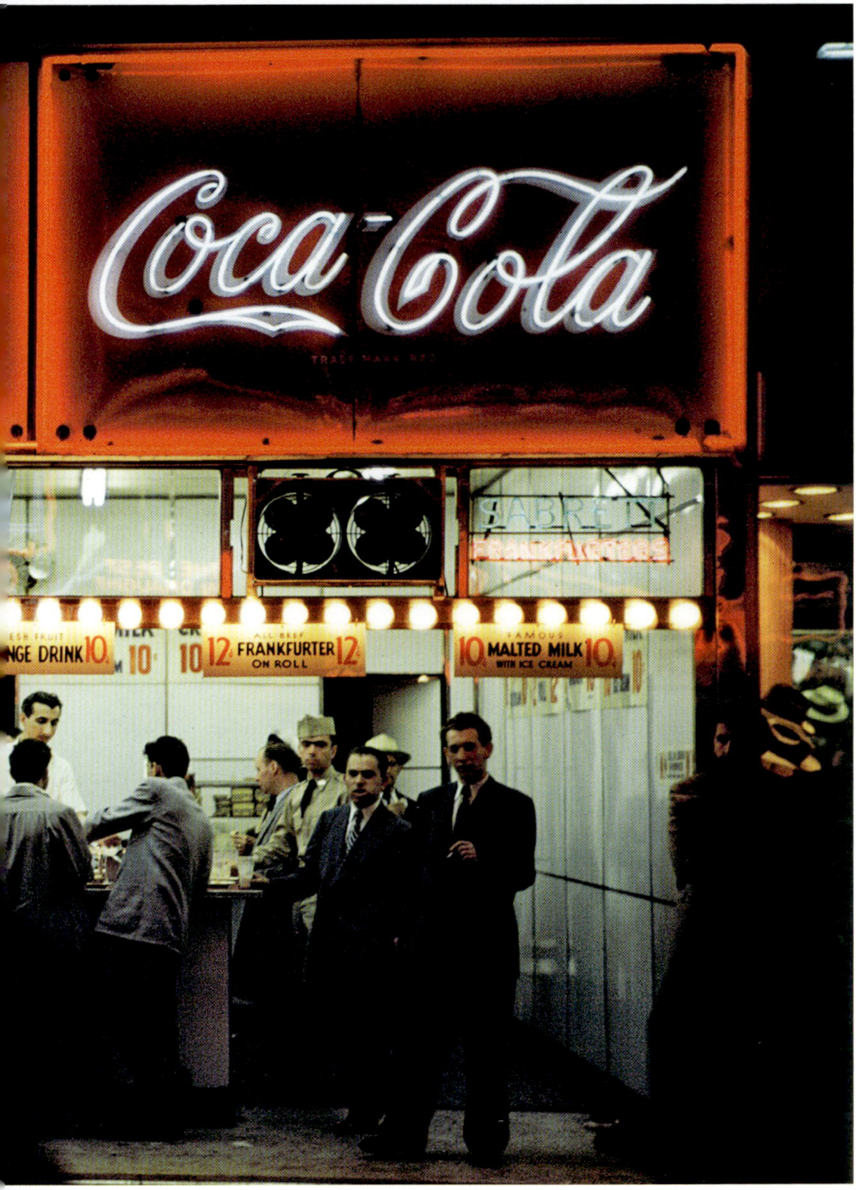

Coca-Cola
TRADE MARK REG.
SABRETT
FRANKFURTERS
FRESH FRUIT
NGE DRINK 10¢
10¢
10¢
ALL BEEF
FRANKFURTER 12¢
ON ROLL
FAMOUS
MALTED MILK 10¢
WITH ICE CREAM

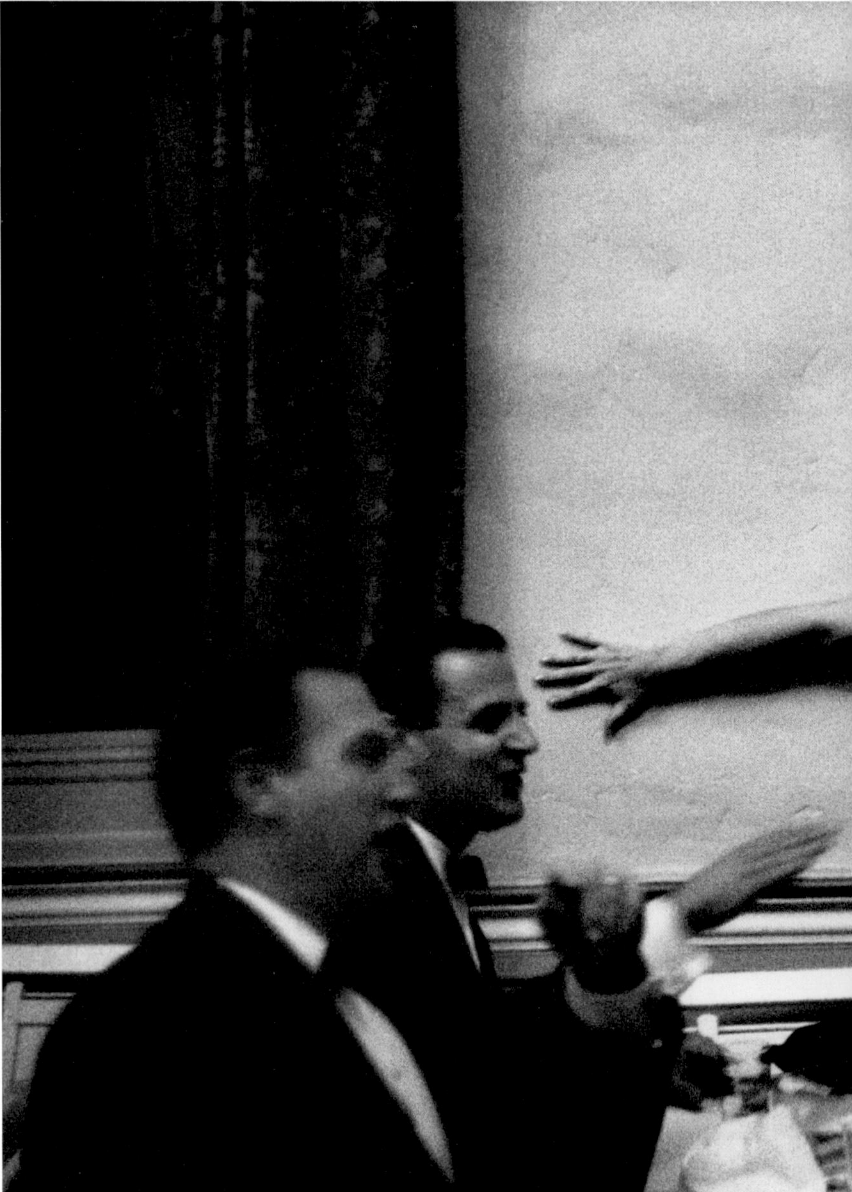

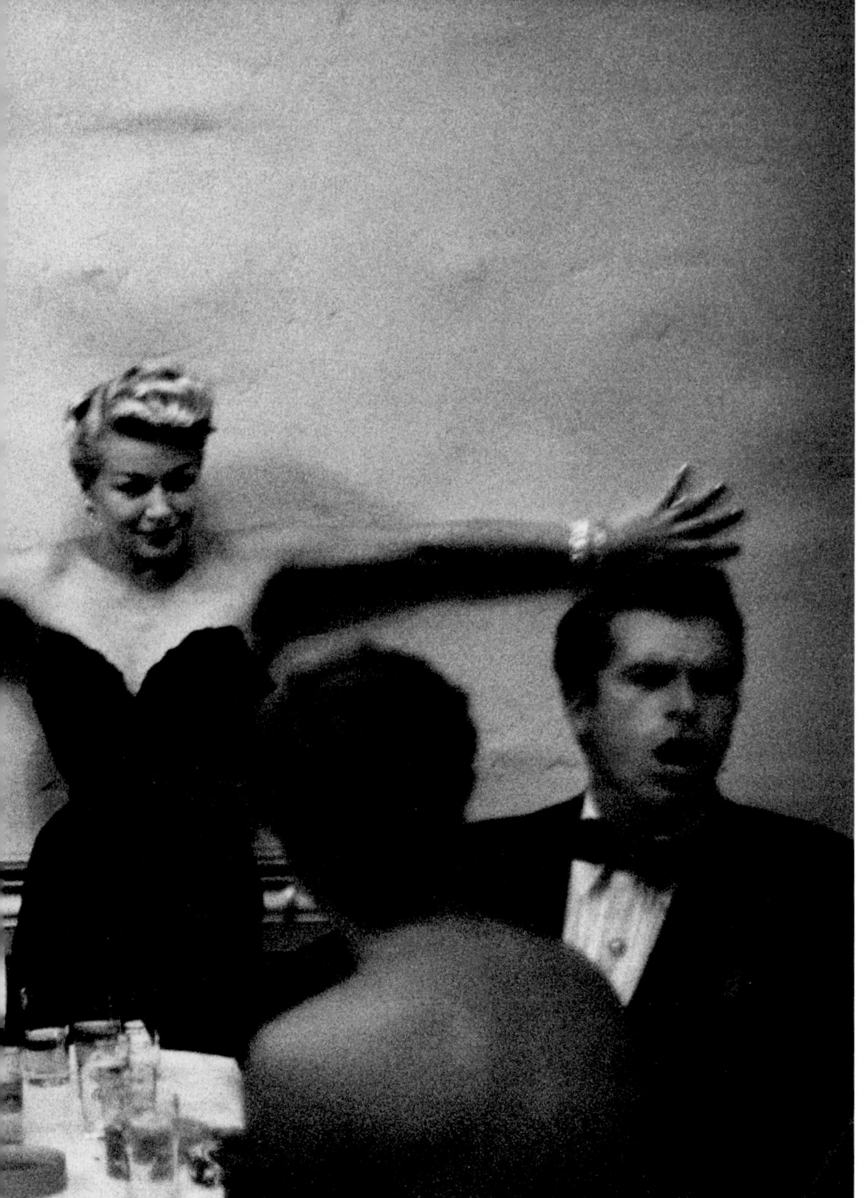

Previous pages:
66. Lana Turner and guests at a party given by Marion Davies,
Hollywood, Los Angeles, 1950.

67. Leonard Bernstein in the green room at Carnegie Hall,
New York, 1950.

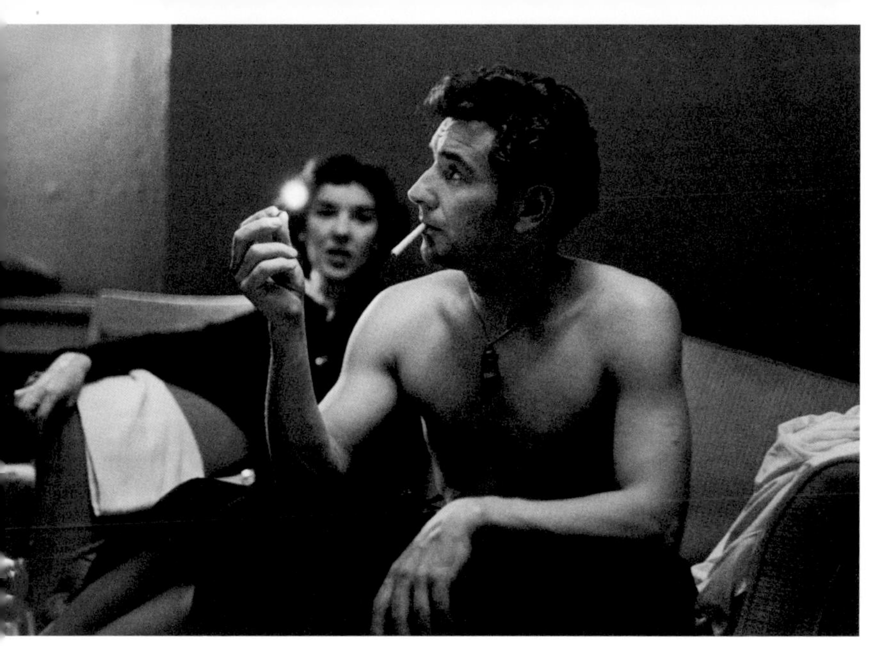

68. Orson Welles at a ball hosted by
Count Carlos de Beistegui, Venice, 1951.

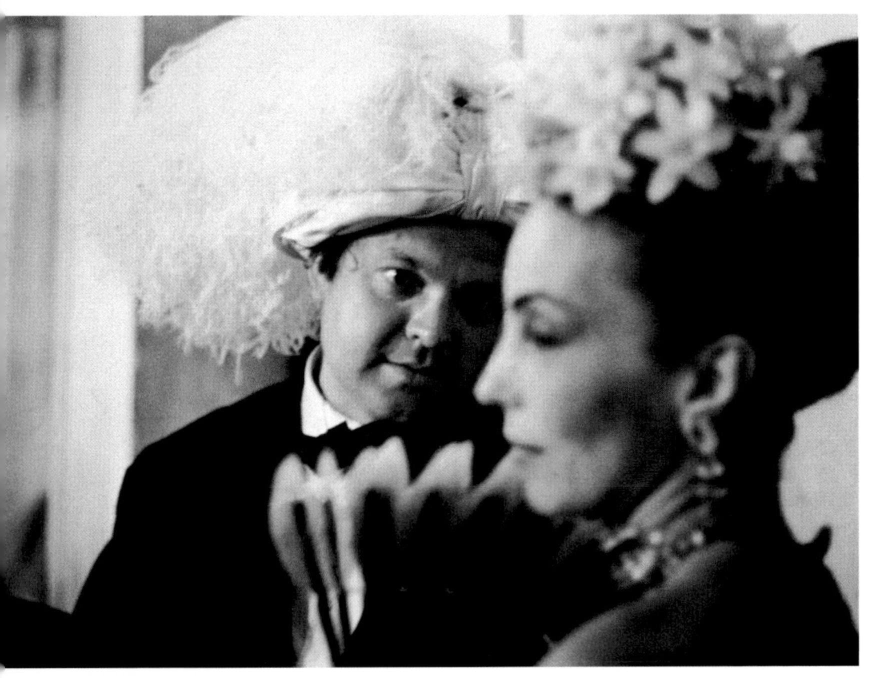

69. Couple in café, Paris, 1951.

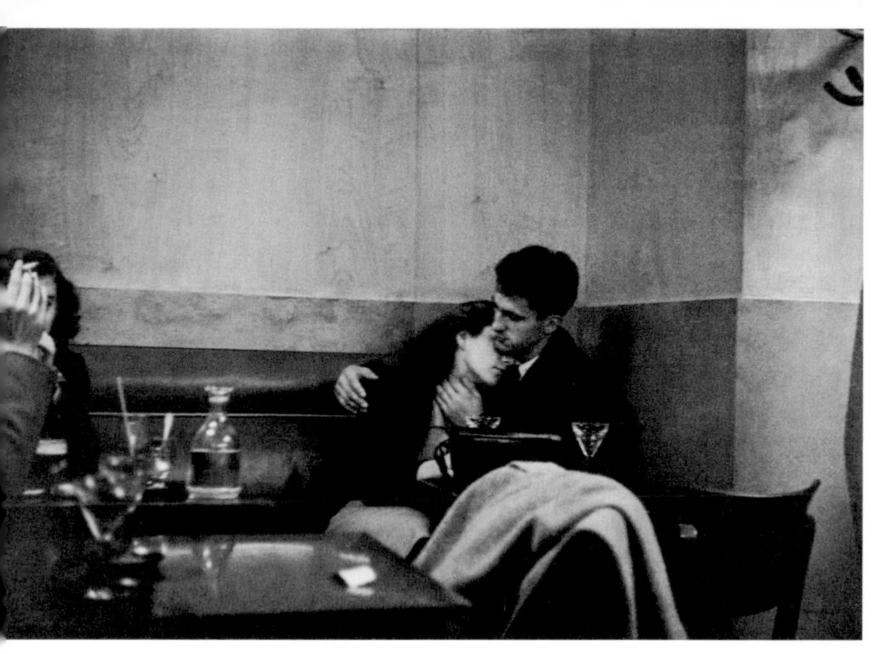

70. 'Family in Arkansas', from the series *Bicycle Trip*, 1939.

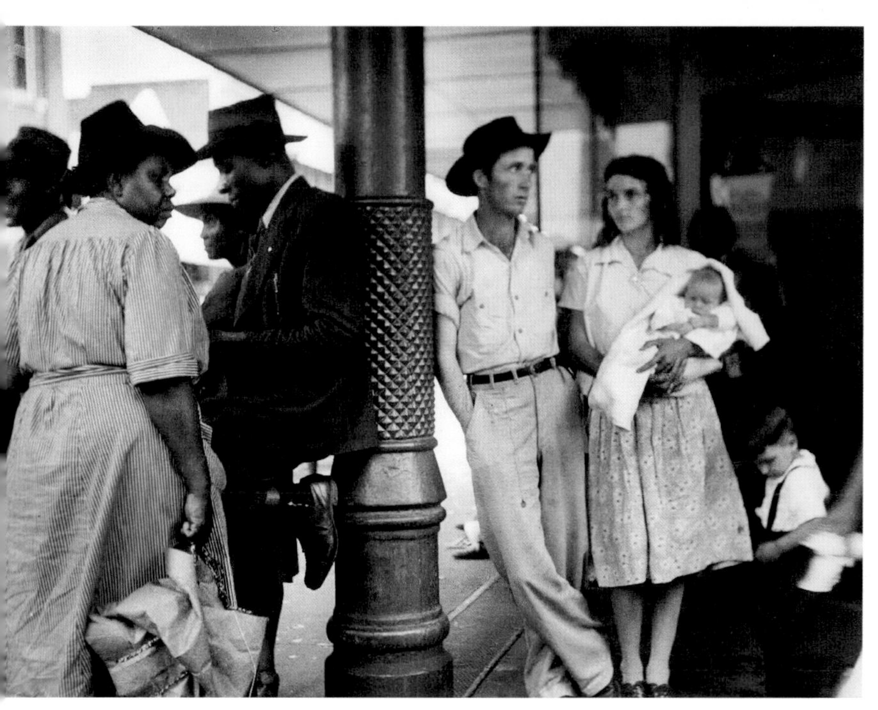

71. Jewish refugees, Lod airport, Tel Aviv, 1951.

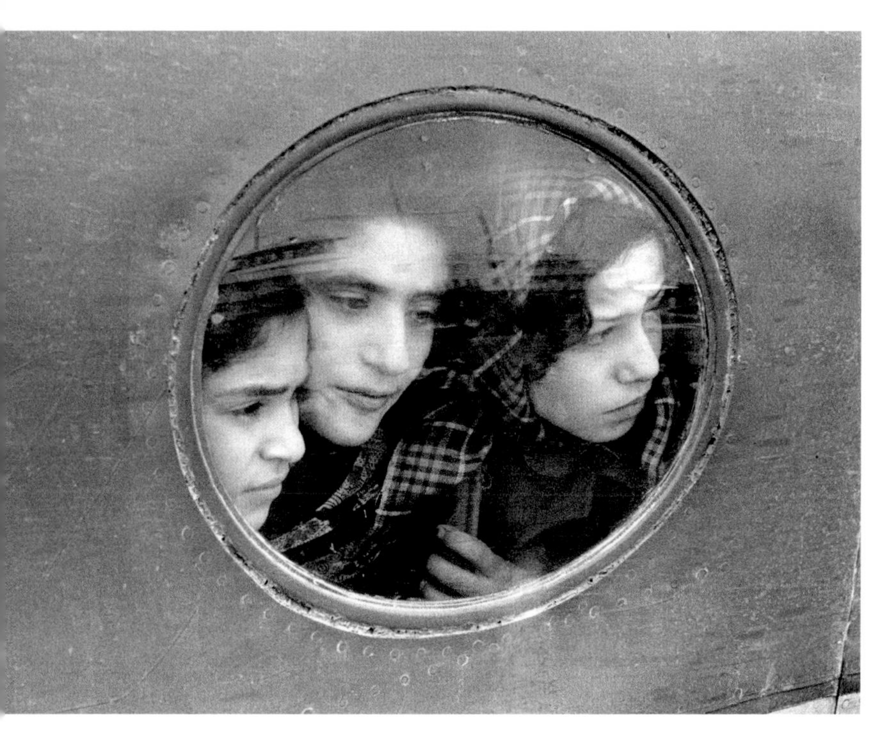

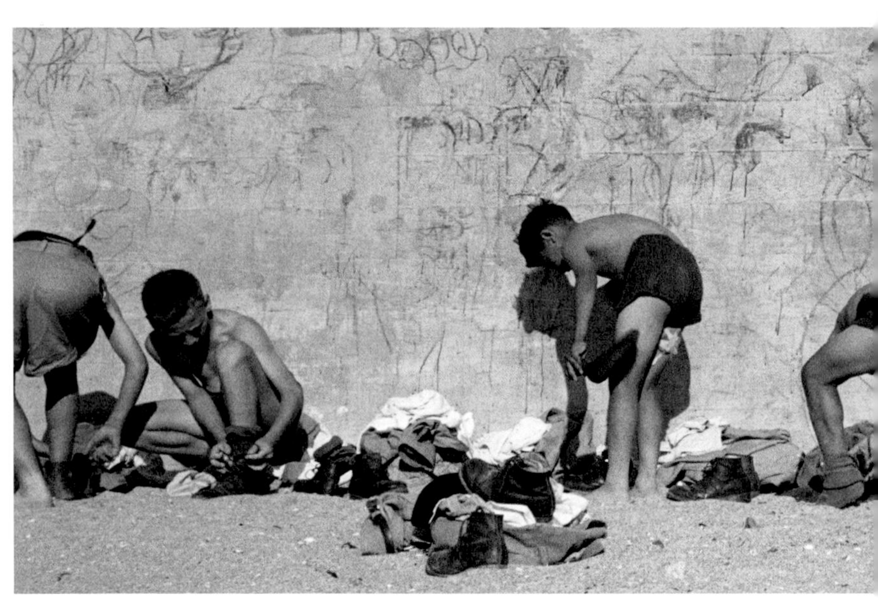

72. Breakwater, Tel Aviv, 1951.

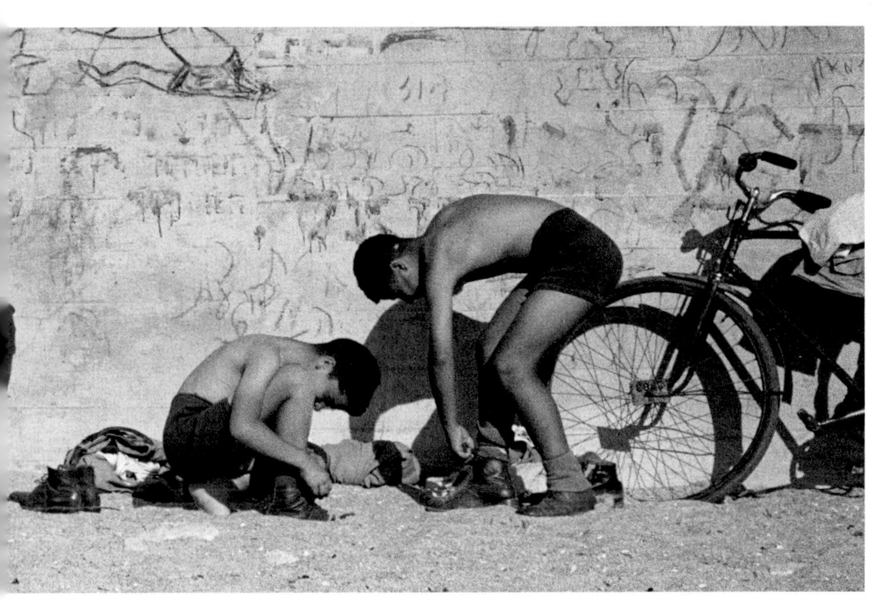

73. Tirza on sinks, Tel Aviv, 1951.

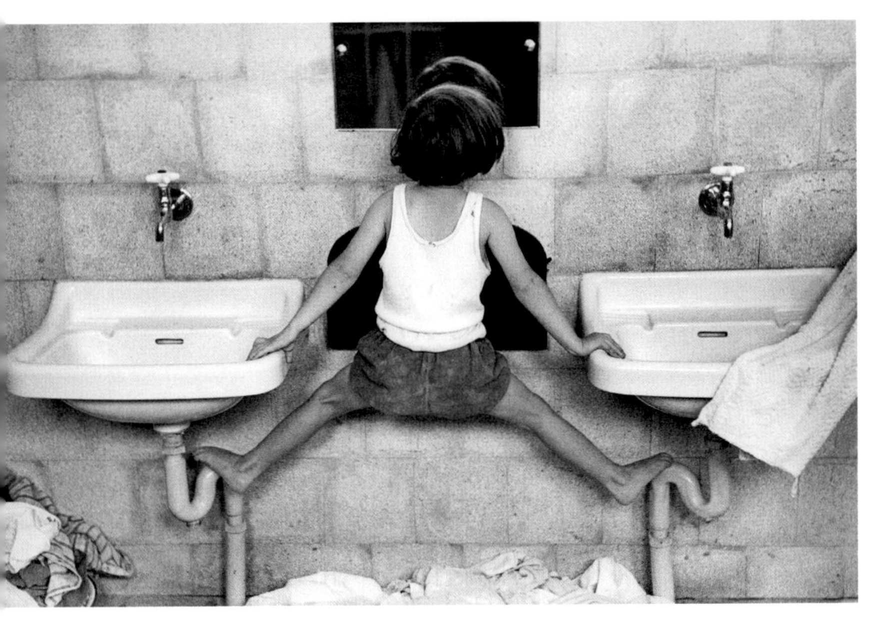

74. Self-portrait, location unknown, undated.

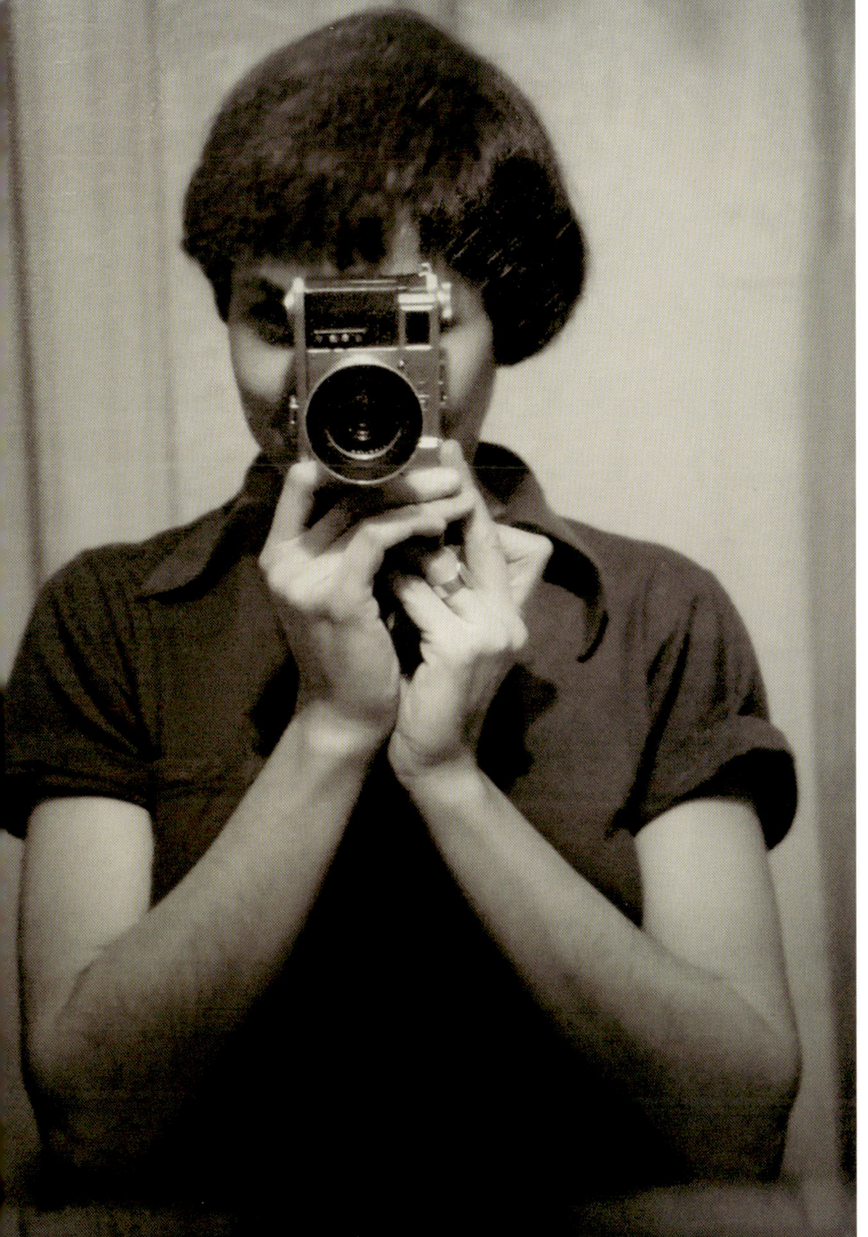

Biography

1921 Ruth Orkin is born on 3 September in Boston. The only child of Mary Ruby, an actress in silent movies, and Samuel Orkin, a craftsman who made model boats, she grows up in Hollywood, already the heart of American cinema. She often goes to film sets with her mother.

1931 At the age of ten, she is given her first camera, a Univex, purchased for the modest sum of 39 cents. She enjoys taking photographs of her schoolfriends and teachers.

1939 At the age of seventeen, she embarks on a long journey across the USA by bicycle, from Los Angeles to New York, to attend the World's Fair. She returns from this journey with hundreds of photographs collected together into an album entitled *Bicycle Trip*, which is reminiscent of the scrapbooks that her mother kept from the films she worked on. This album is, in some ways, Orkin's first storyboard.

1941 She becomes the first female messenger at Metro-Goldwyn-Mayer studios, the legendary production company with its famous roaring lion logo. (Several years later, she will return to MGM to chronicle the working day of another messenger girl at the studios.) She then briefly joins the Women's Auxiliary Army Corps.

1943 She moves to New York, where she works as a nightclub photographer and takes portrait of babies during the day, earning enough money to buy her first 35 mm camera, a Kodak Retina. She starts working for major magazines such as *Life*, *Look* and *This Week*, continuing this work until 1952.

1945 She receives her first commission from the *New York Times*, covering Leonard Bernstein's tour. That summer, she attends the annual Tanglewood Music Festival in western Massachusetts, where she photographs rehearsals and meets figures from the music world including Isaac Stern, Aaron Copland and Serge Koussevitzky.

1951 *Life* commissions her to shoot a story on the Israel Philharmonic Orchestra. She spends six months in Israel, and on the way home she visits Rome, Florence, Venice, Lucerne, Paris and London. In Florence, she meets Ninalee Craig, later known as Jinx Allen, an art student and fellow American, who became the subject of one of her best-known series, *American Girl in Italy*, initially called *Don't Be Afraid to Travel Alone*. The story depicts their experiences as women travelling around post-war Europe alone.

1952 On returning to New York, Orkin marries the photographer and filmmaker Morris Engel. A former war reporter with the US Navy, Engel had joined the Photo League in 1936 before switching his focus to filmmaking. Together, they make two feature films, including the classic *Little Fugitive*, which later serves as the inspiration for François Truffaut's film *The 400 Blows*, a masterpiece of French New Wave cinema.

1953 *Little Fugitive*, co-written and co-directed by Ray Ashley, Morris Engel and Ruth Orkin, is nominated for the Oscar for Best Writing and wins the Silver Lion at the Venice International Film Festival.

1955 Orkin directs her second film, *Lovers and Lollipops*. One of her photo series, *The Card Players*, is featured in the exhibition *The Family of Man*, curated by Edward Steichen for the Museum of Modern Art in New York.

1959 She gives birth to her first child, Andy. That same year, she is voted one of the ten best female American photographers by her peers, along with Dorothea Lange and Margaret Bourke-White.

1961 She gives birth to her second child, Mary.

1965 Some of her images are featured in the exhibition *Photography in the Fine Arts* at the Metropolitan Museum of Art, New York.

1974 The first retrospective of her work is held at Nikon House, New York.

1976–77 She teaches at the School of Visual Arts, New York.

1977 She has a solo exhibition at the Witkin Gallery, New York.

1978 From her apartment on Central Park West, she observes the changing of the seasons through her window, documenting what she sees over the next thirty years. These photographs are collected into two books, *A World Through My Window* (1978) and *More Pictures From My Window* (1983).

1980 She teaches at the International Center for Photography, New York.

1981 Her monograph, *A Photo Journal*, is published, accompanied by exhibitions and lecture tours.

1984 She is awarded the Certificate of Merit from the Municipal Art Society in New York.

1985 On 16 January, after a long battle with cancer, Ruth Orkin passes away in her apartment, surrounded by her photographs and the trees of Central Park, which she loved to look at through her window. Mary Engel founds the Ruth Orkin Photo Archive, dedicated to promoting and preserving the legacy of her mother's work.

Reference section by Tessa Demichel

Selected Bibliography

A World Through My Window, text by Arno
   Karlen, New York: Harper & Row, 1978

A Photo Journal, New York: Viking Press, 1981

More Pictures From My Window, New York:
   Rizzoli, 1983

*Outside: Morris Engel, Ruth Orkin, From Street
   Photography to Filmmaking*, Paris: Editions
   Carlotta Films, 2014

Ruth Orkin: A Photo Spirit, Berlin: Hatje
   Cantz, 2021

Filmography

1953 *Little Fugitive*, 80 mins. (Silver Lion at
   Venice Film Festival, nominated for Academy
   Award for Best Writing).

1955 *Lovers and Lollipops*, 82 mins.

1996 *Ruth Orkin: Frames of Life*, directed by
   Mary Engel, 18 mins. (Sundance Film Festival;
   selected as 'Outstanding Documentary of
   1996' by the Academy of Motion Picture Arts
   and Sciences).

Selected Exhibitions

Solo Exhibitions

1974 Nikon House, New York.

1977 Witkin Gallery, New York.

1978 Milwaukee Center of Photography.
Kiva Gallery, Boston.

1979 University of Akron, Ohio.

1980 Atlanta Gallery of Photography.

1981 Witkin Gallery, New York.

1982 Douglas Elliott Gallery, San Francisco.

1983 Equivalents Gallery, Seattle.

1985 Witkin Gallery, New York.

1990 Photo Gallery International, Tokyo.

1994 Witkin Gallery, New York.

1995 International Center of Photography,
New York.

1998 Irving Galleries, Palm Beach.

1999 Howard Greenberg Gallery, New York.
Jan Kesner Gallery, Los Angeles.

2002 Tom Blau Gallery, London.

2005 Howard Greenberg Gallery, New York.

2007 Stephen Bulger Gallery, Toronto.
Michael Hoppen Gallery, London.

2011 Lumière Brothers Center for Photography,
Moscow.

2014 Duncan Miller Gallery, Los Angeles.
Fondazione Stelline, Milan.

2021 Museo Civico, Bassano del Grappa.

2022 Kutxa Kultur Artegunea, San Sebastián.

2023 Musei Reali, Turin.

2023–24 Mai Manó House, Budapest.

Group Exhibitions

1950 *Young Photographers*, Museum of
Modern Art, New York.

1955 *The Family of Man*, Museum of Modern
Art, New York.

1965 *Photography and the Fine Arts*,
Metropolitan Museum of Art, New York.

1976 *Photographic Crosswords: The Photo
League*, SUNY New Paltz, New York.

1979 *Manhattan Observed*, New York
Historical Society.

1985 *American Images: Photography
1945–1980*, Barbican Centre, London.

1986 *New York: The City and Its People*,
Working People's Cultural Palace, Beijing.

1987 *Masters of Starlight*, Los Angeles County
Museum of Art.
*Master Photographs from Photography in
the Fine Arts*, Metropolitan Museum of Art,
New York.

1996 *A History of Women Photographers*,
New York Public Library.

1997 *Defining Eye: Women Photographers of
the 20th Century*, Saint Louis Art Museum.

2001 *The City That Never Sleeps*, Robert
Mann Gallery, New York.

2002 *Game Face*, Smithsonian Institution,
Washington DC.

2005 *From Within*, Howard Greenberg Gallery,
New York.

2006 *American Photographers: Fine Prints
Exhibition*, Photo Gallery International, Tokyo.

2007 *Women Who Shot the 20th Century*,
Monroe Gallery of Photography, Santa Fe.

2010 *The Heartbeat of Fashion*, International
Center of Photography, New York.

2011 *The Radical Camera: New York's
Photo League 1936–1951*, Jewish Museum,
New York.

2012 *Howard Greenberg, Collection*,
Photo Élysée, Lausanne

2013 *Eye Wonder: Women Photographers
in the Bank of America Collection*,
Cermodern, Ankara.

2017 *The Photo League Exhibition*, Howard
Greenberg Gallery, New York.

2018 *Half the Picture: A Feminist Look at the
Collection*, Brooklyn Museum, New York.

2019 *Your Mirror: Portraits from the
ICP Collection*, International Center of
Photography, New York.

2020 *PROOF: Photography in the Age of
the Contact Sheet*, Cleveland Museum
of Art, Ohio.

The Photofile series is the original English-language
edition of the Photo Poche collection. It was first
published between 1986 and 1992 by the Centre
National de la Photographie, Paris, with the support
of the French Ministry of Culture. Robert Delpire
(1926–2017) was the creator of the series and its
managing editor until 2017.

General editors: Géraldine Lay and Anne Morin,
with the collaboration of Mary Engel, director of
the Ruth Orkin Photo Archive

Series design by Matthew Young

Translated from the French by Bethany Wright

First published in the United Kingdom in 2023 by
Thames & Hudson Ltd, 181A High Holborn, London WC1V 7QX

First published in the United States of America in 2023 by
Thames & Hudson Inc., 500 Fifth Avenue, New York, New York 10110

British Library Cataloguing-in-Publication Data
A catalogue record for this book is available from the British Library

Library of Congress Catalog Card Number 2023939314

ISBN: 978-0-500-41124-7

Printed and bound in Italy

Be the first to know about our new releases,
exclusive content and author events by visiting
thamesandhudson.com
thamesandhudsonusa.com
thamesandhudson.com.au